SALMON FISHING
BRITISH COLUMBIA

Vancouver Island

A 66 1/2-pound chinook caught at Otter Point by Oliver and
Mary Goldsmith out of Sooke Harbour Marina.

THE COVERS
FRONT: Prime coho on a bucktail fly at Campbell River's April Point (See page 82.) **Inset:** The community of Bamfield on Vancouver Island's scenic West Coast. (See page 115.)

BACK: The outer waters of Barkley Sound. A seaworthy boat equipped with CB or radio and reliable motor are essentials for fishing in this area. Fog is common and the nearest land is Japan — several thousand miles away.

PHOTO CREDITS
Campbell River Chamber of Commerce, 9, 78; Cramond, Mike, 102 (top); Heritage House, 9, 63, 120; Nanaimo Tourist and Convention Bureau, 44, 50; Port Alberni Chamber of Commerce, 113; Sooke Harbour Marina, 13; Tourism B.C., 9, 19, 22, 28, 33, 48, 58, 86, 93, 96, 102, 108, 118, 124.

CANADIAN CATALOGUING IN PUBLICATION DATA

Cramond, Mike, 1913-
    Salmon fishing British Columbia — Vancouver Island

    ISBN 0-919214-73-8

    1. Pacific salmon fishing - British Columbia - Vancouver Island - Guide-books. 2. Vancouver Island (B.C.) - Description and travel - Guide-books. I. Title.
SH686.C73 1989   799.1'755   C89-091077-4

HERITAGE HOUSE
PUBLISHING COMPANY LTD.
Box 1228, Station A
Surrey, B.C. V3S 2B3   Printed in Canada

PUBLISHER'S NOTE
As anglers well know, fishing conditions are extremely variable, changing not only from location to location but also from day to day and even hour to hour. For these reasons, this book is a general guide to areas where fish have been caught for generations, rather than a specific one. Similarly, the maps outline the general parameters of fishin' holes. They must not be used for navigation.
    For topical information on local conditions such as where fish are biting, lures to use and best times, the most reliable sources of information are marine gas stations, marinas and sporting goods stores. Don't forget to ask about fishing closures since they can be implemented after the current Federal Fisheries *B.C. Tidal Waters Sports Fishing Guide* has been printed. The onus is on anglers to know where and when these fishing closures apply.

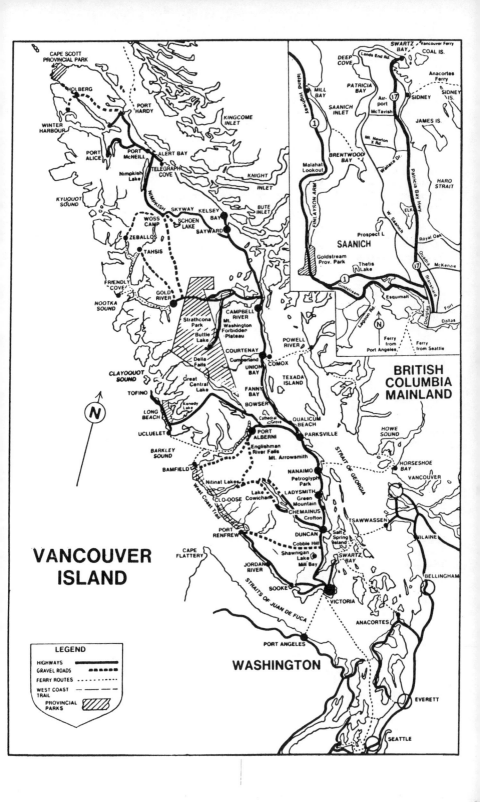

Contents

Chapter 5
CENTRAL VANCOUVER ISLAND
Campbell River

Chapter 6
NORTHERN VANCOUVER ISLAND
Kelsey Bay to Beaver Harbour

Chapter 7
WEST COAST OF VANCOUVER ISLAND
Port Alberni to Barkley Sound

Chapter 8
WEST COAST OF VANCOUVER ISLAND
Ucluelet to Fair Harbour

THE AUTHOR

Now retired after 24 years as Outdoor Editor of *The Vancouver Province*, Mike Cramond has lived in West Vancouver, B.C., for over 65 years. But as he notes: "Hunting and Fishing in my father's footsteps has taken me around the world."

His first published story appeared in *The Shoulder Strap*, official magazine of the B.C. Provincial Police force in which Mike served. Since then he has appeared in national U. S. magazines from *True* to *Field and Stream*, *Outdoor Life* to *Sports Afield*. In addition, he hosted "Hunting and Fishing Club of the Air" on Vancouver's CKWX radio station, the first program of its kind in Western Canada.

His first book was *Hunting and Fishing in North America*, published by the University of Oklahoma Press in 1957. Since then he has written eight more, including *Killer Bears* which became an international best seller with sales of some 70,000. His first B.C. salmon fishing guide, *Fishin' Holes of the West*, sold some 25,000 copies.

In his den are many plaques and awards attesting to his successful career as an author-journalist. They include two National Newspaper Awards, the most prestigious of news writing awards. In addition, there are six of the annual prestigious Cartwright awards for the best in Canadian outdoor writing, two from Evinrude, and 10 National and International awards for features on conservation. At 74 Mike is still writing, his current project updating *Fishin' Holes of the West* which is now out of print.

DEDICATION

For Thelma, whose maps make it legible and whose perseverance made it possible, and in memory of Vic Faulkes.

GLOSSARY

Commonly used among sports anglers is a terminology which is not always constant, even from one town to the next. In addition, there is a jargon which becomes locally fashionable, even from season to season. There are, however, fairly constant terms which apply to most fishing gear and species. They are the ones used in this book. To help avoid confusion, their intended meaning is as follows:

Chinook, or spring salmon, means *Oncorhynchus ishawytscha*, also commonly called tyee, king, or smilie. Chinook is a definition agreed internationally to be interchanged with and for the term king, or king salmon.

Coho salmon means *Oncorhynchus kisutch*, also commonly called silver, blueback and northern.

Chum salmon means *Oncorhynchus keta*, also commonly called dog, keta and dog salmon.

Pink salmon means *Oncorhynchus gorbuscha*, also commonly called humpback and humpy.

Rockfish means any variety of the *Sebastides* family that are commonly called rock cod.

Lingcod means *Ophiodon elongalus*. Of the family of kelp greenlings, it is also called ling. (It is not, however, a true cod.)

Herring, Clupea pallasii valenciennes, or Pacific herring, commonly called bait, strip, plug, firecracker, minnows (by non-West Coasters), and cut plug, among other names.

Grilse: According to Federal Fisheries, "An immature salmon of any species is classified in the sea as a grilse." Since there are size restrictions on all five species of grilse, anglers are advised to check carefully the current edition of *British Columbia Tidal Waters Sport Fishing Guide*.

Bottom fish, or coarse fish, roughly means anything but a salmon. The term includes lings, rockfish, tomcod, soles, flounders, sculpins, grey cod and sablefish.

Dodger means any large attractor at the end of a line between the rod and the terminal tackle, bait, or lure. It includes the term "flasher," unless the particular item is named by brand or type.

Jig means a lure used to cast with and used in a jigging (not snagging) manner. Typical of these are Buzz-Bombs, Stingsildas, Reef Raiders, Strikers, Pirk, and Rip Tide, among others.

Casting lure means any lure which is commonly used to cast with, by any method, but more particularly those which are used in spinning, thread-lining, level-wind casting, or strip casting. (The latter term means stripping line off any reel and casting it from the deck).

Wire line means the use of wire line, either by presentation from a reel directly or by a downrigger.

Downrigger means the use of a large secondary reel with heavy steel line to which is attached a lead weight, usually seven to 10 pounds. The fishing line is attached to the downrigger line by a release mechanism. Consequently, when a fish strikes the angler is able to play it with a light rod and line.

FOREWORD

After 60 years of travel in search of Vancouver Island's fishin' holes, I have merely skimmed the surface of the length of its coastal waters. And though I have flown over and sailed around it many times, I've barely seen all its uncounted bays, peninsulas, sandbars, reefs, islands and islets. Every day in a long lifetime would be needed to fish and discover the hundreds of Vancouver Island fishin' holes along its 2,150-mile coastline, and additional 1,500 miles of shoreline on its tributary islands.

The first European to visit these waters wasn't looking for fishin' holes. Juan Perez, in 1774, was there in the Spanish corvette *Santiago* to chart new coast lines. He was followed in 1792 by Captain George Vancouver aboard HMS *Discovery* — the first person to circumnavigate Vancouver Island.

He wrote of it: "To describe the beauties of this region, will, on some future occasion, be a grateful task to the pen of a skillful panegyrist. The serenity of the climate, the innumerable pleasing landscapes, and the abundant fertility that nature puts forth, require only to be enriched by the industry of man with villages, mansions, cottages and other buildings, to render it the most lovely country that can be imagined."

Unfortunately, the "industry of man" has not enriched some parts of the Island as Captain Vancouver had hoped. Bays are polluted with industrial effluent and major cities such as Vancouver, Victoria, Nanaimo and a host of other communities dispose of their virtually raw sewage by piping it into Juan de Fuca and Georgia Straits. As a consequence, the Federal Fisheries *B.C. Tidal Waters Sport Fishing Guide* contains page after page listing areas where bivalve shellfish harvesting is closed because of pollution, mostly from domestic sewage.

The early visitors, however, didn't have to worry about pollution, and so plentiful were salmon, shellfish and groundfish that they wouldn't have needed a guide book to the fisheries of Vancouver Island. Its many high mountains, reaching to over 7,200 feet on Golden Hinde, rake the moisture-filled clouds from the warm air of the Japanese current to fill the rivers and streams with crystal waters. These flow to the innumerable bays and inlets to create an ideal habitat for five species of West Coast salmon and their feed. Together with the anchovies and Pacific herring stocks (now diminished) there is feed for the salmonids, rockfish, kelp greenlings, cod, flatfish, etc., and the abundant inshore shellfish.

The fishing season is year round, and catches can be from fair to spectacular during the seasons of salmon migration and maturation. Chinook sal-

Hoping for a 50-pounder or larger from Campbell River's world famous Tyee Pool.

Alberta visitor Dick Cole with 21- and 22-pound chinooks from Nanaimo.

On the west coast fronting the open Pacific Ocean, Ucluelet and Tofino are developing into sports fishing centers, services including guided fishing trips such as the one below from a mother ship, the *Canadian Princess*.

mon of 50 to 70 pounds are recorded annually, while cohos, from blueback phase to mature, can weigh in at over 20 pounds — and they are abundant. In the "up" years the pink, or humpback, catches often come in limits, with sockeye also now plentiful in the sports catch. In areas where heavy fishing — both commercial and recreational — has taken place, the stocks of bottomfish are minimal. In isolated areas, however, and on both coasts, it can still be difficult to get a bait to bottom without a species of edible white-fleshed fish taking bait or lure.

All of the southern end of Vancouver Island is accessible by road, from where a car topper or trailered boat can be easily launched. This statement also applies to mid-Island on the Pacific (west) side, and Port Hardy on the inland (east) coast, where the main highway terminates. No matter what part of the Island's coastline the angler-boater goes to, he will find secure harbour almost within an hour's rowing, and most certainly less than an hour in a 6- to 10-knot boat.

Vancouver Island offers a large variety of motels, hotels, marinas, sporting goods stores and similar amenities. It is served by scheduled airlines and the B.C. Government Ferries fleet. Major communities include Victoria, the capital of British Columbia, with a population of some 250,000; Nanaimo, with some 50,000; Port Alberni, 18,000; Courtenay, 10,000; and Campbell River with 17,000. In addition, there are many smaller centers that offer most tourist services. Since anglers make an important contribution to the economy of all communities — large and small — they will find local residents friendly, especially since many of them are anglers themselves.

Many of these anglers provided information during my original research for this book and in the updating. I thank them all. However, without the aid and company of four veteran sports fishermen in particular, the updating would have been impossible. They are Mike Dickey who helped with the Sooke to Saanich data; Nori Nishio in the Nanaimo region; Elgin Six in Campbell River; and George Keary in Port Hardy to Telegraph Cove. To these four a special thanks.

Mike Cramond
West Vancouver, B.C.

P.S. (VERY IMPORTANT): Do not go fishing without first studying the current *B.C. Tidal Waters Sport Fishing Guide*, published annually by the Federal Department of Fisheries and Oceans. It is available at sporting goods stores, marinas and similar outlets. The Guide contains all current regulations governing sport fishing not only for salmon but also for halibut, rockfish, crabs, oysters and other species. Check carefully the sections on spot closures which were introduced to conserve chinook salmon.

Chapter 1

SOUTHERN VANCOUVER ISLAND
Sooke to Esquimalt

Otter Point

OTTER POINT: On the run outward from Sooke Harbour the angler has the choice of either the distant land's end to the west which is Otter Point or, near by, Donaldson Island — locally called Secretary Island. The position of Otter Point is such that it provides a race around either side, caused by tidal flows. Such waters always tend to make fish mill, or feed, and become caught in turbulences which make them vulnerable.

There isn't any real bay either side of Otter Point, but the underwater land rises to form a few hundred yards of shallows from 60 to 120 feet, then falls in the main Strait of Juan de Fuca to depths from 180 to over 400 feet. It is therefore a fair holding area for and deep enough to keep passing salmon migrants on a casual pattern. It is more a coho and pink fishing area than one for chinooks, but the latter do pass through and big ones are taken in good numbers.

Location: Approximately four miles from the ramp at Sooke Harbour, with beach-type access of its own. At Sooke, a fishing port and village, bait, tackle, gas, accommodation, camping, trailer courts, a good ramp and guide service are available.

Where to fish: The point juts into the tidal flow. It can produce salmon on either side and in front, according to water movement. Most angling is confined to within a few hundred yards off shore where there are apparent beaches, but some anglers range a mile out to sea.

The popular method is trolling in a semi-circle from one side of the point to the other, with circles in the downstream flow of the current on whichever side that is. Bucktailing is occasional, as is lure-casting. Strip-casting and anchored fishing, however, are not usual. Mooching is complicated by lack of still water, but drift-mooching is logical.

Gear: Generally the same as Donaldson (Secretary) Island with a stronger preference to deep trolling and heavy gear. Light gear is less productive, but useable, due to the lack of concentrations of fish in a real holding pattern.

Note: Definitely not small boat — 10- to 12-feet — water if using Sooke Harbour or Basin as a port. Okay if launched from the beaches. Winds in Juan de Fuca Strait are generally brisk, rising quickly and subject to local thermal activity. It is a long run back against a sou'easter.

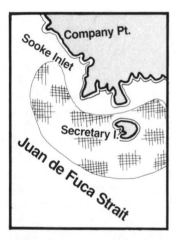

Donaldson (Secretary) Island

DONALDSON (SECRETARY) ISLAND: After threading the twisting passage out of Sooke Harbour past Whiffin Spit, the outer sea buffer, the shelf of Sooke Inlet broadens to the full exposure of Juan de Fuca Strait.

To the east is the rugged promontory of Possession Point, typical of the outer West Coast of Vancouver Island. Adjacent to it the rocky hummock of Donaldson Island creates a small but turbulent inshore narrows. This narrows results in a typical back eddy on either side, according to the run of the tide, which is swift. It is the only apparent island from Otter Point to Little Church, just past nearby Becher Bay. Being set in this long stretch of migrational passage of salmon up and down the big Strait where fresh water flows outwards over major shallows, Donaldson is a logical holding and feeding area for fish. It is a major fishin' hole, favored for big chinooks most of the year, cohos from May to October. Pink and sockeye salmon both provide good catches in season and good years.

July 1 catch at Sooke Harbour Marina, the chinooks ranging from just under 23 pounds to nearly 40.

Location: From nearby Sooke Harbour Marina, and private launching ramp, it is about a half-mile of careful navigation through inner Sooke Harbour to the head of Whiffin Spit, then another mile past it in an outward curve past Company and Possession Points.

Where to fish: The back-eddies created by the tides cause a fairly broad expanse of turbulence up to one-quarter mile offshore and one mile either side of the island. These fast tide lines moving up and down Juan de Fuca Strait flow into both sides of the bay and provide excellent waters for chinooks up to 50 pounds. The area has ideal depths of from 15 to 180 feet, with sheer drops to over 400 feet.

Gulls, murres and cormorants find the feed, and indicate it when turbulence brings it to the surface. Both anchovies and herring surface and jump in the slicks and are a good indication that cohos are around. A frustrating problem is that sea bass and kelp greenlings take the live cut-bait, or lure when inshore near the kelp. In addition, there is a bad underseas reef near the entrance to Iron Mine Bay, and some shallows in the outer area of Donaldson Island.

All and any of this area is top fishing water for either deep troll or surface bucktailing, and excellent for jig-type lure casting.

Gear: The characteristic "weight-on-a-line" rig is used more than any other, and for some reason it occasionally works better than a slip-weight on the nylon. Downriggers directly to the fish are used by the local anglers, some with poles extended to eight feet. Drop-off, or release gear, is the next preference. Planers and dodgers, plugs, bait — cut, whole strip, or slab — with anchovies raked locally being popular.

Bucktailing is occasionally very effective on cohos. Jigging-type lures are used to some degree. Mooching and strip-casting can be effective but are not extensively done. A rod can be a stout trolling piece with a large heavy top guide to allow the beadchain setup to pass directly onto the reel for trolling. (See under Cape Calver for further Gear-to-Use instructions.) Any light, spin-casting, bait-casting or fly-rod formula, mooching-stripping rod also excellent. A good capacity reel of the mooching, drum type is needed for the big chinooks.

Note: TIDES ARE STRONG AND IT'S A LONG WAY TO ASIA in a boat bereft of power. On calm days a 12-footer is adequate, as secure harbour is only a mile off. But always watch the weather.

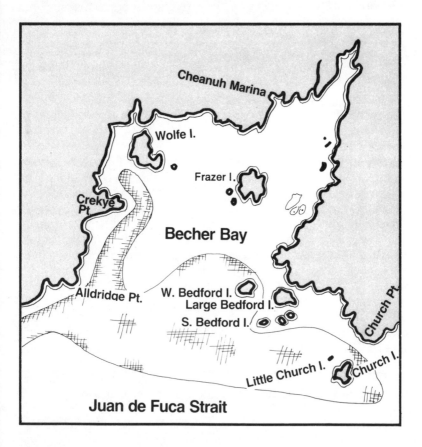

Becher Bay

BECHER BAY: In sports fishing reports, Becher Bay and its adjoining inlet, Pedder Bay, fill the record books of Vancouver Island with large chinooks and cohos. Becher is the more expansive of the two bays with a somewhat greater selection of fishin' holes to choose from.

Next in line from Sooke Inlet, it is on the route of salmon in and out of the large Juan de Fuca Strait. The summer and autumn cohos, pinks and chinooks are the mature salmon runs from their sojourn in the open Pacific, in prime condition and of good size. There are, as in all bays, the wintering immature chinooks from December to June, the mature ones the rest of the season. An early population of smaller resident-type coho is there in June and July, with a high year on pinks every other season.

There are several holes broadly separated. For easier identification, each is described separately.

Location: From downtown Victoria, it is about 17 miles via the Trans-Canada Highway then the Metchosin and East Sooke Roads.

Where to fish: Mooching and drift fishing are productive at or near Frazer Island, particularly during winter months.

ALLDRIDGE POINT: One and one-half miles from Cheanuh Marina and less than one mile from Pacific Lion Marina, the nearest point to the open waters of the Strait. Rocky, with shelving inshore and good salmon depths of 30 to 90 feet. The currents back-eddy on the inflowing tide, creating a wide fishing pattern one-half mile off the shoreline and into the central bay. Anglers begin here if the weather and tides are right.

Location: The inner headland to the west end of Becher Bay.

Where to fish: This area resembles Cape Calver in relative position to Juan de Fuca Strait. It is moderately good bait and strip-casting water from here into Creyke Point. Both chinooks and cohos move in and out of the area. Many trollers move from here in a circular pattern out into the central bay, and across to Bedford Islands and Little Church Islands. Others start their troll from here around the coastline, west to Beechey Head and beyond. It is more coho and pink water than anything else with rockfish, sea bass and lingcod in the bottom reaches.

Gear: Most of the effort in these waters is downriggers or heavy, trolled gear with the lift-off, drop-weight up to several pounds (see Cape Calver). It can be fished, however, with heavily weighted 10-ounce motor mooching gear. The tidal run is fast and almost constant which makes light gear less effective.

Some drift-mooching and lure-casting is done in the entire area, with bucktailing when the cohos are moving past in numbers, and light trolling at the same time. It is an all-type gear area, where light rods and reels are less useful than the medium to heavy equipment. Downrigger and release-type equipment in close to shore is a gamble against the reefs.

Note: The main tides, winds and weather are in full force out on this point and in mid-bay. Boats should be over 14 feet during unsettled weather, and a reliable motor is a MUST.

BEDFORD ISLANDS TO CHURCH POINT: From the outskirts of Becher Bay almost due east the broken shoreline shows three groups of islands: West Bedford, South Bedford and Church. West Bedford Island lies at the beginning of the shallows of the large bay and forms the first exposure to the eddy and strong tides from the main body of Juan de Fuca Strait. This underwater promontory is extensive, and has inner shallows which are conducive to gathering feed. It is in the direct passage of salmon in and out during migration.

Location: This water is the easterly portion of the very expansive Becher Bay. Beginning with West Bedford Island (the inner one) and moving around past Church Island to the opposite side of Church Point, both marinas of the bay are just over a mile, with about the same distance of coastline from one fishing point to the other.

Where to fish: Trollers move directly across the bay from Alldridge Point or Beechey Head, using the inner contour of the bay, thence turning outward at West Bedford, and along the outside of the island groups to Little Church, thence around into Whirl Bay.

More fish are taken in the vicinity of Little Church and Church Islands than in the inner bay because of the strong turbulence of the waters. The large island is favored as a hot spot, with some bait and lure casting possibilities in close where waters run from 30 to 120 feet, then on the opposite side to Swordfish Island, which is an extension of Church Point.

There is an excellent back-eddy type of condition in this area which forms a holding place for salmon and feed. There is some good lure, bait-casting and shallow-water fishing inshore.

Gear: Over much of these waters, which are expansive in the bay, the heavy troll type of gear is most usually used (see Cape Calver) as the tides are strong and more turbulent off the outer points. Dodger with bait such as herring, lures or bucktails are the usual tackle. Some deep lines with plug used, but little of the casting type of gear in outer waters.

Inshore, where reefs will entangle deep tackle, lighter gear is effective and jig, or Buzz-bomb and Silda-type lures produce good results. It is a probable good strip-casting area, with some inner portions open to heavily-weighted motor mooching, cut-plug or activated herring hook-ups.

Note: It is open water on the big Strait, heavily tidal and changeable. Even though the shelter of islands and the bay is fairly close, it is not really small boat water.

BEECHEY HEAD: The focal point of most of the traffic out of Becher Bay is here. Its rocky headland forms a turbulence of waters on both sides, according to the tides, and directly out from it there is a long undersea promontory of 120 to 240 feet for almost one-half a mile. This type of point at the headland of an inlet causes migrant salmon to mill and feed right to the surface. It is also the major producer of the area for three species of salmon: springs, cohos and pinks. The full force of the tidal runs in and out of the inner passage has been charted at seven knots. It is obvious, then, that for this type of water, open to all the fogs, winds and seas of the coastline, a well-equipped craft is necessary.

Beechey Head

Location: Close to three miles from Cheanuh Marina, and just over a mile from Pacific Lion Marina.

Where to fish: All the shoreline from Alldridge Point, past the jutting promontory of Beechey Head, thence around it into the bay with the small islands and even continuously to Sooke's Possession Point. The main catches, however, come off the Point and into the westerly bay.

When pinks are in, the slicker waters off the Point are constantly broken by their jumping. Springs and cohos are in this fast water, but tend to move into either side as the tide changes direction, favoring the back eddies. The waters to the west of the Point can be considered for lure and bait-casting, and deep, heavily-weighted motor mooching. Some drift-mooching with lighter gear is also used.

Gear: Traditionally, the heavily weighted, lift-off drop weight (see Cape Calver) is used with a dodger and lures or bait such as herring, needlefish and anchovies. A heavily-weighted troll of any kind is more productive because of the strong current which predominates most of the time.

The waters are clear, and small lures can be cast in the back-eddying waters on either side of the point, but fast currents and turbulence bring them to the surface. As most of the fishing is for mature fish, and not resident salmon, the most effective gear is heavy to medium.

Note: Don't go to Beechey Head in an ill-equipped small craft or one without a good turn of speed. It is exposed to the worst of sea conditions: wind, tide and fog.

PEDDER BAY: Both the inner and outer bays of these often windy and always cold waters of Juan de Fuca Strait yield salmon.

Location: (See Becher Bay.) The large marina includes a multi-width hard-top launching ramp that goes right down to high tide, with edge tie-up spots. There is lots of parking except on weekends when from four hours after

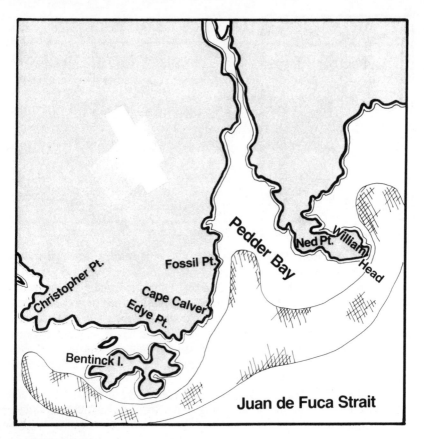

Map labels: Pedder Bay, Ned Pt., William Head, Fossil Pt., Christopher Pt., Cape Calver, Edye Pt., Bentinck I., Juan de Fuca Strait

Pedder Bay

midnight to two hours after sun-up, boats are coming and going and trailer parking is at a premium.

The marina has a good, well-kept rental boat service, gas and oil, tackle, charts and bait. Some guiding services available in the area.

CAPE CALVER: The corner of the rocky shoreline is open to the Strait of Juan de Fuca, with a vista of islands to the south and southwest, a ruggedly beautiful place. Tides race either way past the outer reaches, forming a back-eddy on the flow, or a fast pull on the ebb. At all times the tide race holds salmon.

Location: About a one-mile run from the launching ramp in Pedder Bay, 15 to 20 minutes from Becher Bay where one can see Bentinck Island and the lighthouse off Race Rocks. This area is sheltered from a westerly, except for the wind which comes over the bay off the Sooke Hills.

Where to fish: Anchors hold well at 35 to 80 feet on the underwater shelf near the inside of the kelp bed, and provide some of the best lure casting results on the coast. The general practice is to use jig-type lures from anchored or drifting craft. Running inward along the bay to Manor and Fossil Points (both of which can be as productive at specific times of the tide and day as the outer point), anglers can then drift out on tide and wind, or reverse the process from Calver to Manor on opposing conditions.

From as close as 50 feet from the kelp to 200 yards out, where the shelf suddenly drops to 180 to 240 feet, anchored craft take fish by casting. Strip-casting is not a popular local sport, nor is still or drift-mooching, but both will produce chinooks and cohos as well as anywhere else. Trolling is done from the inner bay, around Cape Calver, and along to Whirl and Becher Bays. Most of the catches come in the vicinity of Calver Point where the waters mill around the underwater shelf. Feed can be seen moving in the bay, along the kelp and well out around the point. Cohos are present from mid-July to late August, with the big northerns into late October. Chinooks are present in large numbers from mid-May to early August, with winter chinooks appearing in October.

Gear: Most of the local boats which troll — and that is the majority — use fairly heavy trolling rods equipped with the traditional large Peetz reel, some with wire line. The more specifically unusual item is the drop-weight principle. It utilizes a two- to six-feet detachable leader on a heavy lead weight (sphere to torpedo) hooked onto or over — but not securely attached — to a bead-chain swivel some 10 to 20 feet up the line from the dodger or terminal tackle. When a fish is brought near enough to the boat, the angler or his buddy lifts this weight off. The swivel then goes through the rod guides

A big reason why Pedder Bay is popular with sports fishermen.

and onto the reel, thus allowing the fish to be brought close, or to fight, without the deterrent of the weight.

These weights start at 1 to 5 pounds (some say 10 pounds) and the reason for them is the 4- to 10-knot tides which are strong enough to lift other weights to the surface, together with the variable, reef-ridden bottom which snags standard tackle like a submarine net.

Beyond the weight, any type of dodger or flasher can be used with strip herring in activators (they are legion), or hooked on to spin. Some anglers use only spinning herring, either large or small, plug-cut or slabbed.

The use of downriggers is not as common as in Georgia Strait, more particularly because of the bottom conditions and the traditional methods, including the already described drop-off weights.

In close, at anchor or drifting, the spinning, bait-casting, stripping or mooching tackle right down to the fly-rod are an excellent choice for sports angling. Jigging-type lures such as Buzz-Bombs, Dart, Reef Raider, Striker and others can be better cast using a fly rod having an extended butt. And, when cohos are plentiful, a trolled fly will — and does — catch fish. Any type of lure which will take a salmon elsewhere will catch them here. From the heavily-fished areas bottom fish such as rockfish, sea bass, lingcod are nearly cleaned out, but present away from the concentrations of anglers.

Note — and warning: Boats under 14 feet are too small for these waters, but occasionally 10 to 12 footers do come out on calm days. Tides reach 10 knots, and few people can row against this current. Fogs move in quite quickly, and wind is always a factor to watch closely. It often rises during the day and drops off from near sundown to shortly after sunrise.

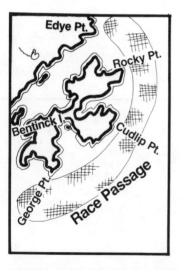

Bentinck Island

BENTINCK ISLAND (North): This island appears to be a part of the mainland portion of Rocky Point until outside Cape Calver, and it is in the same flow of tides and winds. The shoal water between it and the shore is quite shallow, with a maximum channel depth of 10 to 25 feet. This is reef and bait fish habitat, one of the reasons the salmon stay in the area. The outer finger of the conglomerate island is Cudlip Point. It is a focal point for many anglers who venture further out of the bay than the mainland cape, almost in a direct trolling line with Race Rocks.

As in the inner point, cohos and chinooks abound at specific times of the year (see Cape Calver).

Location: Approximately one-third of a mile into Juan de Fuca Strait, abutting Race Passage. The shelf of rock tapers off in width here, and the pull of the tide becomes quite strong, as do the winds. Reached from Pedder Bay, and sometimes Becher Bay, but at the end of the run from the latter.

Where to fish: Cudlip and Rocky Point (on Bentinck Island) have a bay with a pocket of shallows and a generous amount of kelp. Some anchoring is done at the extremity of the bay, where it deepens to 35 feet, then drops to 100, but it is not as comfortable to fish as the inner point. Jigging-type lures are productive. Because the winds and tides are strong, drifting in the area is usually quite fast.

Trollers circle the area between the two points, outward to one-half mile, with the better results being within a few hundred to a few dozen yards. Although the incoming tide is said to be best, fish are there at any time, particularly in the early morning and late afternoon-evening.

Gear: This area is more prone to the use of trolling gear such as described under the Cape Calver section. Jigging types of lures do produce fish when the waters are less disturbed by wind and strong tides.

Note: Weather and tide conditions can be severe, seldom calm. Don't try this area in a small boat unless you are a capable sea hand.

BENTINCK ISLAND (South): Facing right into Juan de Fuca Strait at the extreme end of Race Passage on the landward side, George Point forms a portion of a hooked bay which begins the shallows in behind Bentinck Island. The back eddy from an out-flowing tide forms in this rugged corner with the full force of the constriction of Race Passage rushing by. Although virtually open to the Strait, it gives a lee for fishing and begins a stretch of trolling past Whirl Bay to Church Point and Church Islands.

Location: The opposite end of Bentinck Island, with an even better shelf of rock for holding bait and anchor.

Where to fish: Outward past the finger rocks just off the point, in waters which average 60 to 75 feet, stretching all the way to Church Islands. The best fishing is off the point outward to an invisible reef about 400 yards away. Trolling down to Christopher Point and back in an oval pattern keeps lines in good waters. For times of fishing see Cape Calver section.

Gear: This area does afford anchorage and slow drift waters at proper times of tide and wind, so that cast lures can be used on light tackle. However, the trolling methods described earlier in this chapter are most commonly used — and are successful.

Note: Remember! These waters are fast and changeable with a rough channel through Race Passage if bad weather patterns are brewing.

Southern Vancouver Island abounds in fishing holes — all close to major services. Above are Trial Islands, with B.C.'s capital city of Victoria in the background.

CHRISTOPHER POINT: This is the midland point between the two popular bays of Pedder and Becher. It is also in the full flow of Juan de Fuca Strait, with salmon passing during all their migrations through these waters. It is the usual terminus of most of the boats plying out of harbourage or marina. It is not really a holding place for salmon, due to its position, but capable of creating back-eddies either side which will collect some bait, and thus some feeding fish. The water depths surrounding it are excellent for fishing.

Location: About three-quarters of a mile from Bentinck Island, out of Pedder Bay, with all the same information applicable to both areas.

Where to fish: Both sides of the point shallow off quite abruptly, and do afford anchorage for casting. Drifting is governed by the tide and wind. Trolling is productive in any of the waters out to one-half a mile where depths drop to 200 feet and lessen the chances.

Gear: (See under Bentinck Island. Map on page 18.)

WILLIAM HEAD: Don't go ashore here since William Head is the site of a penal institution. Actually, a more beautiful spot could not have been chosen as a rehabilitation facility if the rocky shoreline jutting into Juan de Fuca Strait is considered. In fact, some trusted prisoners have been known to enjoy casting for salmon right off the point. Latterly, the warning signs to ward off the approach of private craft seem to have been removed. However, remember that a craft may neither get close to shore nor touch land for any reason.

The waters from Ned Point to William Head have a shelf with a variable depth from 25 to 125 feet and this depth extends around the outer promontory into the expansive waters of Parry Bay.

Location: This is the point immediately to the north of Cape Calver, which forms the outer extremity of Pedder Bay, fully exposed to the tides and winds of Juan de Fuca Strait. The run is equidistant from the inshore marina, about two miles; the same from Bentinck Island. (See map page 18.)

Where to fish: Any of the waters in the shelf up to 400 yards off the point, then around it and into Quarantine Bay will produce fish, although to a lesser degree than at the other opposite headland, but at the same times and in the same types.

It isn't advisable to anchor close inshore for casting, but a mild wind and a slack tide will produce conditions conducive to casting jigs, plugs or strip from a drifting boat. Trollers move along this area with some deference to the probability of being warned off.

Gear: This area, due to the prohibitions of the penal camp, doesn't lend itself to light tackle, but the trolling methods used and described under the Cape Calver section do apply.

Note: Don't go blundering into the perimeters of the institution for any reason, and keep a reasonable distance from the shoreline. All wind and tide precautions for the area are the same.

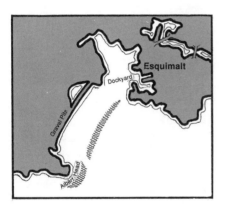

Albert Head
Esquimalt Harbour

ALBERT HEAD AND ESQUIMALT HARBOUR: Albert Head juts well into Juan de Fuca Strait, about 15 miles southwest of Victoria Harbour, and provides excellent salmon and coarse fish catches during most of the year.

Location: As already noted, and about 15 minutes run from the good launching ramp at Fleming Park in Esquimalt.

Where to fish: All the way from Albert Head to the Dockyard in Esquimalt there is excellent opportunity to take fish on both troll and drift fishing.

Gear: Generally the same methods as used from Sooke Harbour easterly, with excellent catches of chinooks, cohos, and, in season, pinks. Main months are June to August.

Note: As are all the areas in Juan de Fuca Strait, these waters are subject to both heavy currents and changeable winds. Small boats in calm weather only.

Chapter 2

SOUTHERN VANCOUVER ISLAND
Victoria to Saanich Inlet

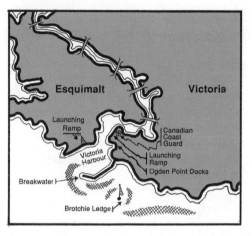

Victoria Waterfront

VICTORIA WATERFRONT: The whole scenic length of the Capital City's waterfront is, during salmon season, used from the shoreline itself and in small and large boats to catch both salmon and coarse fish, with black sea bass (rockfish) angling popular and productive.

Location: Mainly, this area of fishable water lies within the City's downtown sphere, with excellent launching facilities, both at the Esquimalt Fleming Park area, and in between the Coast Guard property and Ogden Point Docks.

Where to fish: Generally, off the mouth of Victoria Harbour itself out to Brotchie Ledge, and along to Clover Point. The large breakwater at the harbour mouth is popularly used in salmon season, with casting directly off the rock walls out to sea. Some casting is done right off the beach, but it is mainly productive for black sea bass and bottom fish.

Gear: If fishing from a boat, salmon fishing tackle is the same as generally used in the area. Breakwater and beach fishing, however, require a good casting rod and reel, the "surf-casting" tackle giving the largest area of coverage. In the latter method, all heavier type lures are predominantly in use. Trolling with heavier gear — downrigger, etc. — is most generally used out around Brotchie Ledge.

CLOVER POINT TO TRIAL ISLAND: The bays in between the points

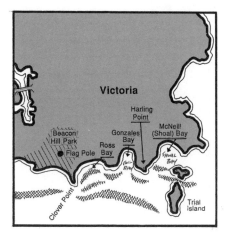

are subject to quite heavy fishing for salmon during the main runs, and do provide a fair number of coarse and bottom fish. This area can be as productive in season as most of the waters to Sooke.

Location: As noted, accessible from launching ramps in Victoria and Esquimalt, also from the Oak Bay ramps and sometimes by portable boat from the shoreline.

Where to fish: All of the Juan de Fuca waters along the coastline can and do produce salmon during their season: chinooks, cohos, pinks, and sockeye. Here drift fishing and trolling heavy are popular methods, with some fair catches made by casting from locations jutting into the current. The back eddies off Clover Point where the kelp is visible are productive and even in the shallows off Ross Bay when the herring and needlefish are there in abundance. It is mainly a summer fishing area, but provides winter chinook catches as well.

Gear: This area is mainly trolling and drifting, with some shore casting. The casting and heavy trolling gear prescribed for the entire area are productive.

Note: If the weather begins to show signs of winds it is time for smaller boats to head back to more protected nearby waters.

OAK BAY: To say that Oak Bay is beautiful is an understatement. The approach to it along Dallas Road increases the angler's desire to get out and fish its reefs, bays, islands, tidal races, shallows and offshore shelves. About five miles from the city centre, the marine drive passes Oak Bay Marina which has all the necessities of angling and boating, including rental boats and charter boats. It is modern, well-kept, and often busy.

Hundreds of anglers use these waters, each with his own choice of fishing hole. It is a May-to-October area for chinooks, some tackle-busters. In August the cohos begin to move in or past in some numbers, to finish in October. Winter salmon fishing is good for chinooks but subject to the area's windy weather and occasional fogs. It isn't as good as it was 20 years ago

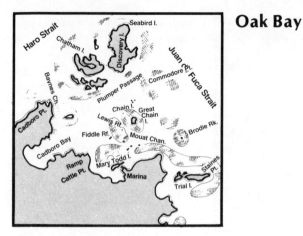

Oak Bay

since there are no localized runs from nearby hatcheries. A competent angler, however, is often rewarded with salmon and some coarse fish.

Location: Along from the marina, nearly to Cadboro Bay, Cattle Point separates Oak and Cadboro Bays and provides the finger for the two well-kept, free public ramps with ample week-day parking for vehicles with trailers.

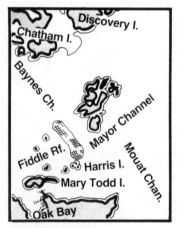

Fiddle Reef

FIDDLE REEF: After leaving the Oak Bay ramps, the first waters of consistent productivity are those surrounding Fiddle Reef, and those which form an intersecting channel between Baynes and Mayor Channels, leading into Mouat Channel. Major fishing craft not wishing to circumnavigate the Discovery Island group use this short cut to Juan de Fuca Strait. The tidal flow is up to three knots and the passage a natural one for migratory fish. There is a small, unattended light close to the channel and water flow. The waters are excellent habitat for feed and forage fish, moving from two adjoining straits.

Most anglers, unaware of the potential of the outer strait, simply pass it by.

Location: Approximately one mile from the ramps on the way south to outer Juan de Fuca Strait.

Where to fish: In a line east toward the nearby Chain Islands the flow of the tide is an indicator of the depths which run from 60 to 100 feet heading into Mayor Channel. All of this water is ideal for both cohos and chinooks, the back-eddies and races of currents governing the concentration of effort. The water on the Baynes Channel side is deeper.

It is ideal for drifting and excellent for trolling with light tackle but a little fast and busy for anchoring. The inner bay side is shallow and good right up to the nearby marina. Mary Todd Island and Harris Island can be included in the specific nearby spots with Fiddle Reef as the end of the triangle, often providing the best fishing.

Gear: Most of the inner bays have reefs and shallows, both expected and unexpected, which will grab up tackle, both cast and trolled. Around Fiddle Rock the light gear used for casting will handle any weight which is logical to put down to troll, thus a spinning, bait-casting, or heavier fly rod is indicated. Jigging-type lures are popular and must nearly have paved the bottom by now!

Cohos and grilse move through the passages, so light tackle is effective. Not much strip-casting or drift-mooching is done, but both take fish. Trolling, as noted, is possible if the channels are known.

Note: One of the really quite safe areas for a small craft since the distance to some form of land is short.

Discovery Island

DISCOVERY ISLAND: On the Plumper Passage side of this typical rock-bound inner island there is a channel through the group behind the Juan de Fuca face. It is shallow, filled with rocks, reefs and kelp — ideal for marine

The popular island- and reef-studded waters of Oak Bay, served by Oak Bay Marina, near right center, and two public ramps.

life, (hard on props of the careless) — and it flows into the big Strait. In front of this water the salmon move in and can be found at all tides in their season.

On the outward face of Discovery Island, Seabird Point has a commanding lighthouse which can be seen for miles, a deep-sea navigational aid. Around this point the full force of Juan de Fuca Strait meets Haro Strait, which links up on the other side of the Gulf Islands with Georgia Strait. The Point is thus on the direct passage of the salmon runs via the Juan de Fuca migration route. Like all such tidal and windswept waters, it is "on" or "off."

Location: Sometimes called the "Gap," the area on the Plumper Passage side is extensive along the 60- to 120-feet length, of the whole passage, but productive where the tide line shows between the land groups, and halfway to Commodore Point. Taking the outward point of Discovery Island, using the easily visible lighthouse as a focal point, the tidal flows run strongly both ways forming back eddies. These are the fishin' holes.

Where to fish: In the "Gap" along the face of the major opening in the group of islands. At the lighthouse in a semi-circle on both sides of the light, beyond the kelp on the 50- to 100-feet shelf up to 400 yards offshore.

Gear: A short distance offshore, in Plumper Passage, the depths run 90 to 120 feet, thus any heavy tackle to 90 feet depth will work in trolling — but there are invisible reefs to hang up on. The drop-weight type of terminal gear described in full under Cape Calver section is used, and any other lighter type of dodger-planer set-up will work, herring-to-plug as lures. Most of the area is shallow enough to use jigging-type lures, thus a light rod and reel, spinning to level wind, drum or fly, will handle the area. During the influx of cohos, bucktailing is productive, as can be drift-mooching or strip-casting. Tides are fairly strong and continuous.

Note: It is a long way to the inner bays, so watch the weather. As in the case of the Chain Islets, the entire perimeter of the group of islands which make up this conglomerate can and does produce salmon.

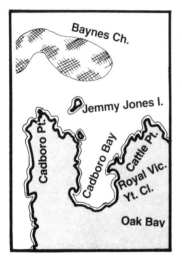

Cadboro Point

CADBORO POINT: Cadboro and Oak are twin bays side by side, with Cadboro Point being their bulwark to the inside passage of Haro Strait, the major landward side of Baynes Channel. Cadboro Bay, with its private Royal Victoria Yacht Club basin, and facilities for affiliates, is a well-sheltered bay in almost any weather, with room for anchorage. The public ramps at Cattle Point, the land division of the two bays, serve it.

Location: Upwards of one and one-half miles northeast of the launching ramp where Baynes Channel separates the headland from the island group.

Where to fish: Beginning at Jemmy Jones Island, there is an underwater bay which cups into Baynes Channel as ideal retaining water for bait. For this reason, with its strong currents from the passage, it is likely to have salmon (always grilse) at any time or tide. This pocket to the point, and around the point into Haro Strait to the next jutting tip, is considered to be the more productive. Near the kelp there is shallow water which drops off sharply to 60 to 90 feet. Anchoring is possible, but subject to strong tides.

Gear: Trolling around the hump of Cadboro Point is feasible with any gear, but hazardous to tackle inshore because of close-to-the-surface reefs.

Casting lures, strip-casting and drift-mooching tackle are all possibilities, with gear as light as fly equipment when the cohos are surfacing. Chinooks also lurk in the deeper areas and throughout the passage.

Note: These are not really sheltered waters, but are safe enough for well-managed smaller boats.

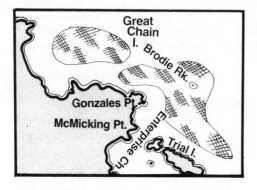

Trial Islands
Chain Islets
Brodie Rock

TRIAL ISLANDS: These rocky picturesque islands with the commanding lighthouse look like a point of no return after setting out on the broad waters of Juan de Fuca. The low-lying land separated from the major land mass by Enterprise Channel is the westerly outward point visible from a boat moving seaward from Oak Bay. It is in the full force of the tidal run of the big Strait, and is a focal point for many anglers. Times of the salmon runs are those mentioned under the Oak Bay section.

Location: Nearly three miles from Cattle Point launching ramp in a southwesterly direction, marked clearly by a lighthouse. Also accessible from the ramp in Victoria Harbour about four miles away.

Where to fish: From inside Gonzales Point (the Golf Course) across the mouth of Enterprise Channel, but there is a drop-off to 60 to 90 feet in a line with Fiddle Reef. All of this is water in which a lure can be cast, a light troll proving effective.

Gear: Off-shore 300 yards a troll can be used to the depth of 50 to 80 feet, but hidden reefs snag deep tackle. Casting gear, spinning rod to fly rod, will handle much of this area. Drift-mooching, strip-casting, lure-casting are all workable methods here.

CHAIN ISLETS: Bounded by Plumper and Hecate Passages to the east, Baynes and Mayor Channels on the major landward side, and Juan de Fuca Strait on the outward reaches, Chain Islets and Great Chain Island have exposure to an abundance of natural fishing waters.

The main and commandingly larger of the islands, Great Chain, is the destination of most seaward-bound anglers once they head for Juan de Fuca Strait. The smell of guano on a hot summer day makes its identification simple.

On the Juan de Fuca side of the Island, a large shelf of submarine rock pushes outward over a mile. With depths 60 to 120 feet stretching between Discovery Island on the northeast, and Trial Islands to the south, this is a major fishin' hole.

It is typical coho traverse, yet holds enough inshore feed to keep chinook, both immature and migrational, in its waters. For dates of probable runs, see Oak Bay section.

Where to fish: The whole area is trolled, and also produces well for the lure, jig or bait caster. The outward edge of the shelf, one mile out, seems to handle most of the trollers as there are depths in the 120- to 210-feet range.

Lure-casting anglers run up-tide or wind and drift over the entire area with good results. Much of the concentrated effort in summer months is just after and including dawn, then ashore until the dying sun and into the twilight. A busy time at all ramps.

Gear: This is an area where the bulk of the catches are on the Juan de Fuca side of the islands, with somewhat less success when circling the group. Trolling gear, up to the heaviest types, is used in the offshore reaches, and lighter casting gear inshore.

Trolling plugs, lures, herring of all cuts work well, as do the jigging-type lures. Count the latter lost if you touch bottom without an instant retrieve. Herring cuts used in mooching, drift-mooching and strip-casting also work quite effectively.

Note: This is fast water on large tides, windswept and open in stormy weather. Don't stay around in a small boat if you see either tide or wind rising.

BRODIE ROCK: Well out to sea from Chain Islets, almost in the waters surrounding Trial Islands, a perceptible change can be detected on the surface of the sea — a definite changing of currents, a riffle which seems incongruous with the expanse of waters surrounding it.

This condition is caused by an underwater reef, its peak some 20 feet under water and several hundred yards in circumference in a near circle. It is a well experienced tackle grabber, a master at the "fooled ya'" strike which tears gear overboard to the surprise of even veteran anglers. The only indicator of its presence — a slick when there is a riffle on the water, or larger waves when there is a slight wind opposite to the tidal flow — can be obliterated by lack of tide or a slight wind, but it is perceptible to the mariner's eye. Waters don't act that way unless disturbed from above or beneath. It is, as most such reefs, a fish collector. The shallower depths are conducive to marine growths and marine organisms which attract herring and needlefish, which in turn mean salmon, rockfish, lings — even the unwelcome dogfish.

Location: The chart shows it is nearly in a line between Commodore Point on Discovery Island and Staines Point on Trial Islands, with a south-southeast heading from the tip of Gonzales Point. In plain talk, go right out to sea until you can look at the islands on either side of the bay and drift toward Trial. But take care — or your deep lines will contribute to the coffers of the "tackle grabber."

Where to fish: As mentioned, from out at sea drifting towards Trial,

31

circle 400 yards around the peak of Brodie Rock with a preference to the side upon which the tidal currents are perceptible to the eye. Look for a rip, back-eddy, needle-point or haystack wavelets which do not bear a reasonable consistency with the surrounding waters. Try the shallows toward Trial Islands on the outgoing tide. Cohos hang in the turbulences. The same indicators and conditions also apply on the opposite side.

Gear: It isn't usual to anchor on the reef, but it is feasible. Thus, any of the jigging-type lures, a strip-cast or drift-mooched herring of any cut, a one and one-half ounce swivel weight with six-feet leader, and small, or needlefish cut-herring will take cohos, or near surface chinooks and grilse. Circling with a bucktail fly on the troll works during the seasonal salmon runs. Shorten trolling gear to 50 feet, or 4 ounces, in the close vicinity, but the heavy troll, dodger and lure with slip weight is excellent in the outer perimeter. It's an all-round fishing place.

Note: It is turbulent here when other areas are nearly calm. Because of the tidal flows being fast, a lure hooked in is likely to be lost. Take care! You are in the full flow and weather of Juan de Fuca Strait.

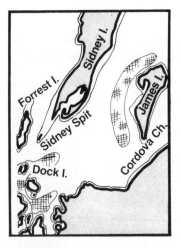

Sidney Island (Spit)
James Island

SIDNEY ISLAND (Spit): Almost due east out to sea from the Vancouver Island shoreline at Sidney, the larger island of the same name cuts off the view of Haro Strait. At its north end, extending about one mile from the mainland mass, there is a long sandspit embedded with pilings which have the incongruous appearance of a picket fence at sea. The spit ends in a small hummock which points directly at Dock and Coal Islands. The low-lying promontory doesn't look like a probable place to hold either salmon or ground fish, rockfish, lings or kelp greenling, but it is a major producer for the area. On the Spit is excellent Sidney Spit Marine Park with wharf and landing floats, picnic and camping facilities.

On the point, marked by a light, the sandy beach shows in line with the

Sidney Island with its prominent landmark, the sand spit at upper center, and anchorage for popular Sidney Spit Marine Park.

pilings, and the run of the tide up Sidney Channel on the west. Miners Channel on the east comes directly from Haro Strait, which is a salmon migration route. Sea birds and feed fish in the shallows along both sides indicate why some holding pattern is established. Local anglers say it is best in evening and morning, but it will produce on the inflowing tide.

Location: Those used to the site of the old boat launching ramp at Sidney will find it paved over. There is, however, an excellent new ramp with good parking facilities in the south end of town, next to the Anacortes Ferry dock. An "Honor Box" is in place to accept the $3 launching fee. Sidney has all services from fuel and marine supplies to excellent accommodation and scheduled airline service, and is a Customs point of entry for visiting U.S. boaters.

Where to fish: The point has an inshore back-eddy which is ideal for bait and lure casting with moderate tidal flows which move the craft over fishing water. Inner Sidney Channel is favored because of the better feeding grounds on the shoals which are formed by the big bay on the westerly shoreline.

A long finger of shoal is quite shallow but drops off on the Sidney Channel side to ideal 60- to 120-feet-deep waters. Trolling is done all along the shoreline to the first marker down Sidney Channel, often a turn-around spot. Miners Channel is more commonly fished nearer the point and across to Forrest Island.

Gear: Moderate tidal flows offer excellent bait- and lure-casting waters. Jigging-type lures are commonly used with success for chinooks, cohos and coarse fish; thus any light type of spinning, mooching, bait-casting rod and reel is sufficient. Most of the bottom is clear of reefs, allowing any type of

33

trolling gear, but heavy gear is not a necessity due to the moderate depths of the channels. Water is clear and dodgers are efficient on all gear, with some bucktailing.

Note: Nearby Sidney Harbour and Sidney Spit Marine Park provide excellent shelter. The run across the bay to the Park, however, can be choppy.

JAMES ISLAND; The first southeasterly land blocking the channel view from Sidney is James Island, which splits Cordova from Sidney Channel, and forms the alternative fishing area from Sidney Spit. It is a low-lying island with fairly deep water right off its shoreline both into Cordova and Sidney Channels. The Sidney Channel side has a slight hook at the extreme southerly end which forms a holding pattern for salmon, thence deep water out to the extensive shallows of James Spit.

Location: Equidistant from Sidney Harbour (closer from Bazan Beach shoreline launching) with Coal Island, it offers the first alternative in direction; about one and one-half miles to the light on Cordova Channel. Sidney is an ideal base since it has all services from bait and gear to lodging and food.

Where to fish: The first point east is considered to be the best water as it is on Sidney Channel salmon migrations, but is not a holding area. Thus further travel is required onward along the face of the Island past its end, along James Spit. Waters average 60 to 120 feet.

Gear: It is primarily a trollers' route, with some casting in the hook near the southeasterly end. Any type of gear, from quite light for bucktailing when fish are moving through (cohos from July to October), to heavy when chinooks are immature and semi-resident in the bay between the islands.

Note: It is close enough to land to make a short run in rough weather and has good lee on the Cordova Channel side.

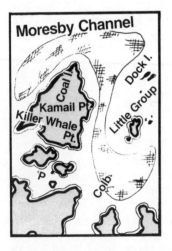

Coal Island

COAL ISLAND: Looking northwest from the seafront of Sidney, the small islands and rocky reefs intervene in a panorama of moderately sheltered Gulf Islands with Coal Island at the nearer outward point. Its shore forms a bay which is to some degree bounded by the Little Group Islands and those intervening in Page and John Passes which connect to the major Colburne Passage leading into the B.C. ferry terminal at Swartz Bay.

The Island has shallows from Killer Whale Point to Charmer Point which holds small feed and many water birds. Between it and the Little Group is a deeper passage, excellent for rockfish and lingcod. Charmer is the rocky promontory — the vortex of Shute, Moresby and Prevost Passages — where tide-races run both ways in an almost direct line to Active Pass. That places it in the migratory route of salmon, but it is neither a summer nor a fall holding water for cohos, chinooks or pinks. It is a better winter and spring area for immature chinooks, and some grilse or cohos.

With at least twenty reefs and other waters to choose from between Portland, Moresby, Sidney and James Island, it is possibly the best alternative.

Location: Under two miles from Sidney, it is the first large island in an almost magnetic north direction, passing the Little Group Islands and many rocks and reefs. The waters are sheltered, but must be carefully navigated in a deep-draft vessel.

Where to fish: From Kenai Point to Charmer is best on an outflowing tide, thence out to Dock Island. On the inward flow the face of a nearly straight shoreline to Moresby Channel can be better. The point itself is probably the best place for casting-stripping type of fishing and to circle while trolling, or trolling in a line toward Dock Island.

During winter and spring chinooks tend to hang closer to the inner end of the Island in the false bay between Curteis and Killer Whale Points, and in the passage between the Island and the Little Group.

Gear: Although strip-casting bait and lure-casting gear can be productive during winter and spring, the lack of consistent holding patterns of migrant salmon makes it a hit-or-miss effort. Trolling covers more ground in fairly deep water off Charmer Point to Dock Island, and will accommodate the deeper downrigger, lift-off, or release-weight type of gear.

Inward the reef pattern can snag gear, and lightweight equipment is better. Dodger and lure or bait is a normal procedure with some drift-mooching and lure- and bait-casting. A composite tackle area, light to deep.

Note: With the degree of shelter, inlets, passages and alternate lees in wind, smaller craft are quite safe. Take a good look back as you leave Sidney so as to locate your point of departure.

SAANICH INLET: This very large, cliff-faced inlet in the Saanich Peninsula comes to within a few miles of the centre of the City of Victoria. Its water depths exceed 600 feet centrally, but become shallower on the approach to Satellite Channel.

Perhaps it is its depth, and the backwater stillness, which breed the big "man-o-war" jelly fish which are noticeable immediately upon boat launch-

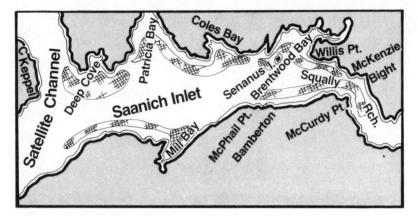

Saanich Inlet   Bamberton

ing, from egg-yolk size to cloudy centred giants over 18 inches across with long stinging tendrils. Although there is not much fresh water moving into the big Inlet, the small herring seem to abound where the current is light.

In the Inlet the salmon seasons are sharply defined. It is not a passing-through point of migration. In the spring the bluebacks show in good numbers. Immature chinooks hold in the deeps during the winter months, and are the object of probably the first and largest wire-line sports fishery on the coast.

The reason is that the 600- to 800-feet depths graduate quite slowly up to 180 to 300 feet along both coasts of the fjord, giving trolling depths just off-shore of 100 to 300 feet, a natural level for chinooks. In such deep waters the resistance from nylon lines requires one to five pounds in order to troll the lure at such an angle that it will reach those depths. Wire — which at one time was chiefly Monel, a costly nickel alloy product — has given way to stain-less steel, or other metal alloys. It is commonly used in the area, with some-times caustic criticism of nylon fishermen that: "Those wire-line bastards will cut you off — keep clear of them!" However much justified the comments, note that wire-line fishermen can be found in the areas of Bamberton to Mc-Curdy Point, and on the opposite shoreline from Willis Point to McKenzie Bight; also in circumnavigation of Senanus Island which takes the course through the outward cup of Brentwood Bay. However, the whole Inlet lends itself to trolling the lengths of both shores, past and into all mouths of the numerous bays.

In July, cohos appear in small numbers as do chinooks, but the build-up of better mature salmon fishing usually begins in mid-August and continues into October. There are a fair number of rockfish, lings and other coarse fish, but because of the narrowness of shallower shoreline shelves, the Inlet is not a prolific breeder of these species.

Location: From the Saanich side the approach is roughly 15 miles to Brentwood Bay, where there is an excellent marina and supply complex, with gear, bait, gas, oil, provisions, a large government dock and ferry landing. A narrow road into the Indian reservation leads to Tsartlip Campsite, which has a modern low-tide boat ramp and a fair but rustic parking area for a number of cars and trailers.

There are also launching points at Brentwood, Finlayson Arm, Mill Bay and Maple Bay, of varying types from natural to a derrick lift.

Note: Individual points, or holes, are treated separately where such a classification is helpful.

BAMBERTON: The shore installations of the old Bamberton cement plant remain plainly visible, and are the reason for the area's name. They are immediately apparent directly across the inlet from the launching places and harbour of Brentwood Bay. The cliffs of this fjord drop sheer to the sea, then continue downward. Only a few yards offshore the line can go down 100 feet, then 300 a few yards further out, then to 600 feet. These sheer depths make it the downrigger and wire-line trollers Mecca because the chinook run deep in these waters.

This is a year-round spring salmon area, with cohos as a lesser concentration during much more limited seasons.

Location: About two and one-half miles from Brentwood Bay, five from Mill Bay. The usual approach is from Brentwood, although there is a marina at the east end of the Inlet, accessible from the Trans-Canada Highway.

Where to fish: The reach is about three miles of precipitous coastline, starting at McPhail Point to McCurdy Point, which is at the entrance to Squally Reach.

Boats often begin at the former site of the cement plant, troll to the first land promontory which is Sheppard Point, then back. Or, go in the opposite direction in a pattern along the shoreline, ending at McPhail Point.

It is difficult to say what attracts salmon to this murky water but, like Britannia Beach in Howe Sound, a small creek comes into it, having depths in front with good results on large chinooks. Perhaps more fish are taken in the down channel bend of the coastline than in other parts of the stretch.

Gear: This is downrigger and wire-line water where most boats cruise slowly with very heavy gear, trolled at depths using planers, dodgers, plugs, spoons, cut and whole herring and hoochies. Any deep trolled gear has a chance.

Note: It is often windy but has moderate tides. There is no lee on this side. A run of two miles to safe harbour should be kept in mind.

DEEP COVE: On the south abutment of Saanich Inlet, where the long fjord adjoins Satellite Channel, the first harbour of Deep Cove indents the Saanich Peninsula with typical forested, rockbound shoreline. This bay, about three-quarters of a mile wide, extends between Coal and Moses Points, with the dot of Wain Rock in a direct line from the latter point. Although Wain Rock is the center of most fishing effort, all points have their own characteristics. For this reason they will be treated separately in this section.

More of the coho, or through-strait migrations of salmon, occur in this

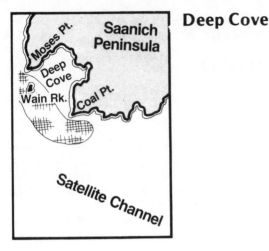

Deep Cove

area, as its waters meet those of Satellite Channel. The presence of grilse is almost constant year round. All seasons may be slightly earlier than the inner bay.

Location: Deep Cove is another six coastal miles further along the Saanich Peninsula, and has its own tiny port with gas, some provisions, bait and tackle.

WAIN ROCK: It is the small blinker-lit rock, outward-bound to the main channel. The tidal flow is constant around it, not too forceful, but excellent for creating turbulence which invites grilse and cohos, and brings herring to the surface.

Where to fish: On the outward face there is a shallow shelf which extends into Satellite Channel. Anchoring is onto rock bottom, which is quite good for strip-casting, jig-type casting, or for drift-mooching of strip herring. The inner face is similar, with similar results, but both changing with the tide. Trollers cruise right around the island, as there is a deep passage between Wain Rock and Moses Point.

Gear: Vancouver anglers would consider this to be a hot spot similar to Scotch Fir or Egmont Points, where both strip-casting at anchor and drift-mooching are done. Light tackle such as spinning, bait-casting, right up to pure fly rod and bucktail outfits are ideal. Trollers can utilize any type of gear as there is 100 feet of water in most of the area, but there are reefs in close to Wain Rock.

MOSES POINT: This Point can be included in the Wain Rock area since most effort occurs within the line from the Rock to the outer edge of the Point, and along Satellite Channel. The passage between the two points is also productive. Tackle and gear are similar.

COAL POINT: The first inward-bound point on the way to Patricia Bay, still close enough to Satellite Channel to be included in its fishing description. It is rocky with a quick drop-off to 60 feet.

Where to fish: It is an open point, which has some anchorage in close, allowing bait-, jig- or strip-casting, and the tides are moderate enough — if there isn't too much wind — to encourage drift-mooching or casting.

A common line of trolling takes in Moses Point, past Wain Rock, across the outer portion of Deep Bay, then to Coal Point, and returns via the outer perimeter of Wain Island, always in fishing water for chinooks and cohos. At times the cohos move in and make this Point the hot spot.

Gear: Identical to that of Wain Island-Moses Point, with a tendency to trolling.

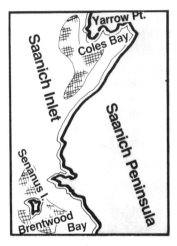

Coles Bay
Yarrow Point
Senanus Island

COLES BAY-YARROW POINT: The hook of Coles Bay faces toward the other productive water of Brentwood Bay. It is formed by a long, low finger of submarine land which juts almost due south for a mile and is marked on its outward line by a black spar buoy. Waters at that distance out are, at points, less than 15 feet but they provide an excellent bar for small herring. There are rocks near Yarrow Point which indicate an unexposed reef and the buoy is the marker on it.

Location: Approximately three miles from the inner bay of Brentwood, outward-bound on the same side.

Where to fish: From the black spar buoy, the underwater reef points directly toward Senanus Island. The waters of the inner side of the reef, which are the outer reaches of Coles Bay, form a pocket from 60 to 120 feet which is both deep enough to hold chinooks and shallow enough to attract coho. Although a near circle into the bay, and out almost on a reverse path, keeps tackle in deep water, the continuity can be reversed once past the outward side of the black spar, then along the coast into Patricia Bay.

The 50-foot depths just south of the reef are excellent waters for bait, jig-type casting and drift-mooching. This shelf extends into Coles Bay. The southern area of the pocket receives much of the fishing effort. Grilse abound around the reef. (Carefully check current Federal Fisheries *Tidal Waters Sport Fishing Guide* since size restrictions apply.)

Gear: Although most fishermen troll, they use less of the wire-line tactics and more of the normal, moderately-heavy trolling tackle for chinooks but light to medium tackle when the cohos have moved in. Some bucktailing is done.

Off the reef conditions are ideal for strip-casting and jigging-lure type of fishing. Anchoring is possible almost anywhere. Drift-mooching also will work since tides are moderate, as will trolling bucktails.

Note: It takes a little adjustment to the fact that the reef comes so far out to sea with consistent shallow water. Stay close to the drop-off.

SENANUS ISLAND: From Brentwood Bay toward the outer reaches of Saanich Inlet, the small island of Senanus appears in the northward path. It is an underwater pinnacle rock with extreme depths immediately off its rock-bound shoreline. There is also a tiny second pinnacle on the outward corner as a reef, coming to within 30 feet of the surface, a tackle-grabber type.

Location: In the entrance to the natural salmon-holding pattern of Brentwood Bay it is, as most such islands are, a good possibility to attract bait, and thus salmon. Visible from the Tsartlip launching ramp, about one mile out, one-half mile from Henderson Point, up inlet.

Where to fish: The depths on the chart indicate a shallower shelf of 120 to 300 feet which corresponds with most of inner Brentwood Bay. A pattern of trolling along this shelf is productive for salmon: some cohos, mostly chinooks. As it is not a logical holding place, it is not particularly suited to mooching, casting lures or jigs, but when the fish are there it does produce.

Gear: Basically a deep trolling circle is required to cover the entire outer perimeter, thus heavier gear or downrigger is preferable.

HAGAN BIGHT: Sluggett Point offers the lee which forms the inner portion of Brentwood Bay and the harbour. From it, outward to the north, the jut of Henderson Point forms the bay known as Hagan Bight.

Deep water is only 100 yards offshore, except for a niche at the Indian reservation where Hagan Creek enters. Perhaps it is this small trickle of fresh water which attracts the herring, then the chinooks, a common coastal combination of habitat.

Location: This is the curved bay into which the Tsartlip launching ramp enters, bounded by Sluggett and Henderson Points.

Where to fish: Although some jigging-lure or other casting type of fishing is done, the stretch can be trolled lengthwise point-to-point and produces fish anywhere.

Gear: This is a natural trolling body of water, with no real holding places to keep salmon in position for long. Thus, although light gear can be used for

Hagen Bight
Willis Point

casting, mooching and bucktailing, the preference is to deeper tackle in a nearly unobstructed path.

Note: This is ideal water for fairly small boats, protected with anchorage and harbour nearby.

WILLIS POINT: The residential quality of the area is typified here in the homes on the water's edge. Instead of a suburban carport, they have a boathouse with a slipway leading into the water. Rocky, but approachable coastline bays are common, and all have their complement of herring breaking the surface in the rather mild current slicks. Such is Willis Point, at the extreme southern tip of Brentwood Bay. It is a natural for chinook mooching, with cohos moving past in their season.

Location: About one mile from the Tsartlip launching ramp, due south past the inner harbour and ferry terminus at Brentwood Bay village.

Where to fish: Waters drop right off to 120 feet (ideal chinook salmon depths) on both sides of the point and into Brentwood Bay, and in the other direction past Whittaker Point to McKenzie Bight Bay.

The troller can cover this entire length of coastline with a deep line. The moocher, strip or jigging-lure caster has a good chance right at the Point, on either side into the bay, or at Whittaker Point.

Gear: As the waters are not fast moving, even on the largest of tides, the area lends itself to mooching (which is seldom done), drift-mooching or jigging-lure type of casting. Strip-casting is feasible though not much practiced.

Most of the gear is deep troll, either downrigger or wireline, with the miscellany of dodgers, plugs, cut-plug herring and general deeper salmon-fishing methods.

Chapter 3

SOUTHEAST COAST OF VANCOUVER ISLAND
Cowichan to Nanaimo

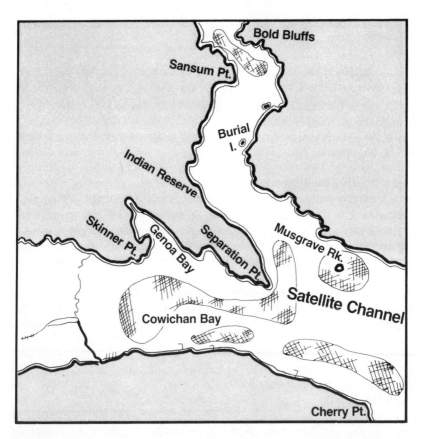

Cowichan Bay   Separation Point   Bold Bluffs

COWICHAN BAY: Early in the century the Cowichan River, one of the largest on Vancouver Island, had one of the most prolific and broadly distributed salmon and trout runs on the Pacific Coast. It even had plantings of Atlantic salmon and European brown trout, the former stocking unsuccessful. It still has major chinook, coho and pink runs, as well as fair dog salmon. The Tyee-type chinooks, for which it was once famous, and the larger late cohos are still there in diminished numbers, but the big sports fishing derby days are over.

The broad expanse of the bay and its shallow waters produce both a good bucktailing season in September and light-weight troll fishery for the mature chinooks (now rigidly controlled by fishery regulations) in the estuarial waters. Bucktailing is still productive off its entrance during later summer and fall.

Location: This Bay is the harbour and mill site for the city of Duncan on Highway 1 where accommodation, gear, food, lodging, bait and most amenities for the sports angler are available. There are lodges on the bay, some rentals and fishing guides.

There are four launching areas, three marinas, and a public ramp at the outer corner of the bay.

SEPARATION POINT: Usually the angler will head directly for the outer end of Genoa Bay, and there begin to troll, mooch or bucktail for salmon. As this rugged headland, with the lighthouse on it, pushes well out into Satellite Channel and forms the first portion of Sansum Narrows, it is in the path of migrating salmon and in a nursery area for their grilse.

It is an excellent area of tidal currents for cohos and chinooks which stay in the deeper waters along the inshore, sometimes off the point. The main run of larger cohos and chinooks do not move in until late August and continue until November, but there are good chances on resident-type cohos from June on, as well as some immature of both species in grilse form.

Where to fish: For chinooks, mooching begins in the harbour, out from the log booms, and along the wall past Genoa Bay. Best results are along the drop from the bay, closest to the point itself, then out around the point and close in.

Cohos move around the point in a full pattern and right across the bay to Cherry Point, with the better production closer to Separation Point, and up the channel between Vancouver Island and nearby Saltspring Island. Tides are fairly strong, but not too fast for drift or motor-mooching. Jigging lures will produce in any of this water, as will light-weight trolling with flasher and bucktail, or one-half ounce weight and spoon, strip or bucktail. Some mooching is done using a bobber, almost unique to this area.

Gear: Although much of this water is in the 120- to 240-feet depths, it does produce well on lesser-weighted tackle. Use of the downrigger and lift-off weights are common, but not as necessary as it is in Brentwood Bay and the Sooke, Pedder and Becher Bay areas.

Bucktailing was, and still is, a common method on cohos in the whole area, with bait- and lure-casting increasing. Jigging-type lures will produce inshore. Light, medium and heavy rods and reels all come into use, depending upon the angler. Mooching is not a heavy competitor but it does produce. Small, colored spoons and all bucktails produce, with the best early colors being red and orange.

Note: It is one of the safer, small-boat areas from the Cowichan Bay side.

A variety of public and private launching ramps, marinas and
Marine Parks such as popular Newcastle Island at Nanaimo contribute
to the popularity of Vancouver Island's salmon fishing.

BOLD BLUFFS (Sansum Narrows): This projection of Saltspring Island
into the waterway is the narrows of the major passage called Sansum Narrows,
which is actually a channel. Elevations on the Saltspring side rise quite steep-
ly to Mount Sulivan, 2,070 feet high. The Narrows are located in the inner
passage along the Vancouver Island side of Saltspring Island, with the major
waters of Stuart Channel pushing from one side, and those of Satellite Channel from the other. The flow of the tide is noticeable and strong, similar to
that of Active or Porlier Passes, but much narrower in extent.

When the coho move through, they hug the Bold Bluff side of the waterway, and are in a confined pattern. On the right tide, flowing up into Stuart
Channel, fishing can be hot, even from the rocks on the point itself.

Location: Bold Bluffs are fished from Cowichan and Maple Bays, with
the latter being closer. Maple Bay has a small ramp beside the wharf in the
centre of the village, with fewer available supplies and provisions than
Cowichan which is about two miles away around Octopus Point.

Anglers from Cowichan Bay and the Gulf Islands can reach it via the
Separation Point tip of the bay, where it lies about four miles distant from the
inner bay.

Where to fish: Because of the inward curvature of the southern narrows
toward Saltspring Island, the best tidal and holding conditions are on this side.
Burgoyne Bay shoreline is less productive, but can be good on the proper tide.
Centrally in the Narrows, the full flow on an incoming tide will produce cohos

as early as July. There is a fair number of bluebacks early in the year in the whole area.

Strip-casting, either from the boat or shoreline rocks, drift-mooching, and some bait and jigging-type lures at peak seasons from July until October. Both sides of the point and in the bays produce chinooks.

Gear: This is a light-to-heavy tackle area where, in season, cohos are generally near the surface. Strip- or bait- and lure-casting rods and reels are adequate. Bucktails behind dodgers, or surface fishing with light weight, also work. It is a typical inside passage fishery with fewer of the big fish likely to be taken.

Note: The tide is fast in the Narrows, but it fans out quickly on either side and can be handled in a small boat.

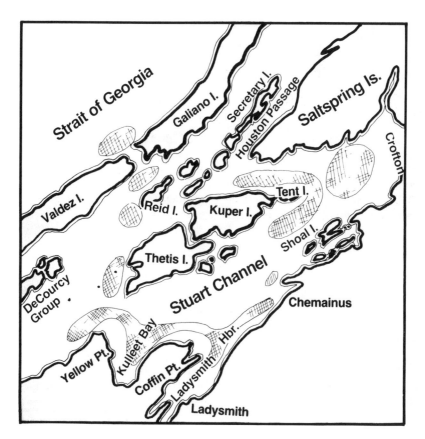

Crofton   Ladysmith   Chemainus

CROFTON: This small town is situated on a slope of land overlooking Osborn Bay. Being close to Sansum Narrows, Thetis, Tent and Kuper Islands and Porlier Pass, much of the angling effort gravitates in those directions. It is a first report area of blueback-coho catches and has a fair, immature chinook record during the winter months.

Location: Off the Trans-Canada Highway via either Duncan or Chemainus. The town has its own sports shops and most other services, including bait, gear, gas and, in mid-town, a good ramp at medium to high tides, poor at low water.

Where to fish: Local anglers say the area of the outfall of the nearby mill is the best for chinook and this condition can be all year round, with good mooching in the winter and spring months. The water between Osborn Bay and South Bay (Vesuvius) on Saltspring Island in the centre of Stuart Channel has a large blueback-coho population from April to early June.

Gear: Light gear is excellent, as mooching for springs is successful, and immature cohos (bluebacks) are taken on the surface troll.

CHEMAINUS: The free Kinsmen launching ramp, which is just north of the centre of the mill town, keeps busy most of the year with local use alone. Most of the anglers immediately head for Thetis, Tent or Kuper Islands, or Porlier Pass, which can be reached by fast boat in 10 to 20 minutes across waters with usually temperate wind and wave conditions.

However, beginning at Bare Point (a long finger which encloses the harbour), a stretch of shoreline extending to Ladysmith is favored by trollers.

Location: The small town lies off Trans-Canada Highway 1 on the shore road, either from Duncan or Crofton on the south, Ladysmith or Nanaimo on the north. It has all services of a company town — gas, provisions, tackle, accommodation. There are harbours nearby if the local one is busy.

Where to fish: From Bare Point to Boulder Point is just over two miles of shoreline, with some inshore reefs near the launching point, then a good trolling depth along the drop-off of 60 to 90 feet. Most of this water is possible chinook salmon mooching area, but it is open and has no well-known or defined holes.

Off Bare Point and the shallows west of the ramp, there are deep waters which do hold chinooks and more immature winter and spring fish. These areas are subject to some lure- and bait-casting for fair catches during the earlier seasons, but not much doing on cohos at any time. Local anglers who know the area troll deep lines, further out, to pick up cohos at as much as 100 feet.

Gear: Trolling is the locally popular method, with anglers using anything from light troll, dodger and fly on cohos, to downriggers for the larger chinook.

As the waters have little tide the results from either mooching, strip-casting or jigging-type lures are productive.

LADYSMITH: From any of the four access points to the saltwater in this lumber town, it is only five minutes to the fishing areas. In fact, the bay of Ladysmith Harbour is a central point of effort. With 35- to 120-feet depths almost constant between Boulder and Coffin Points, the area is ideal as immature chinook holding water, with some mature migrants in the fall.

Location: The first town south along the main Trans-Canada Highway 1, about 12 miles from Nanaimo. The public ramp is near the wharf, and amid the booming grounds there are three others. All services: bait, tackle, provisions, accommodation and fishing resorts are nearby.

Where to fish: The central area of Ladysmith Harbour can be productive of chinook all year round, with a better early fishery than a late one. Trolling is begun centrally, and out around Sharpe and Coffin Points to Kulleet Bay, and on to Yellow Point. Watch your deep gear from Sharpe to Coffin Points, as the reefs extend past the buoy on Coffin Rock directly out from the point of the same name.

Gear: Much of the local effort is trolling, but water depths are conducive to light tackle, with some mooching and lure-casting practiced successfully.

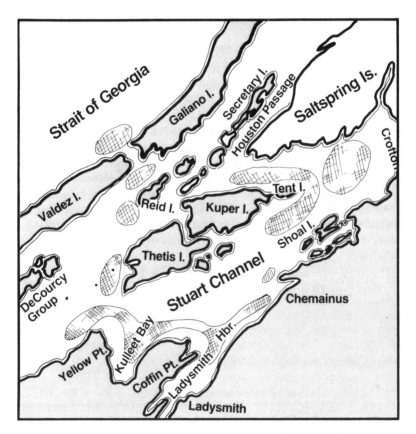

Thetis   Kuper   Tent Islands   Yellow Point

THETIS, KUPER AND TENT ISLANDS: Basically these three islands and Porlier Pass receive the brunt of local sports fishing effort from Maple Bay to

At Ladysmith productive fishing water begins in the harbour and extends in all directions outside the mouth.

Nanaimo, with moderately productive winter fisheries and some seasonal migratory salmon arriving after August from Crofton, Chemainus and Ladysmith Harbours.

The last three communities have ramps which are within three to four miles of the westerly shore of one of the islands, and almost the same distance from the eastern side to Porlier Pass. Local anglers in all three places consider the Porlier Pass fishing the only dependable all-season fishery, but acknowledge that there is a fair winter fishery for immature chinook and a good blueback pattern of fishing in April and May. This condition is typical of a nursery fishery where fair, small feed is available, but where there is no heavy migrational pattern of salmon to a larger river system.

Location: These Islands are bordered on the Vancouver Island side by Stuart Channel, separated from the main line of Gulf Islands bordering Georgia Strait by Trincomali Channel and Houstoun Passage. They can be reached from the ramp at Crofton which, although generally fair, is poor at low tide (but free); the excellent mid-town ramp at Chemainus (also free); or four Ladysmith entry points, public to private type with services of gas, oil, food and fishing supplies, with accommodation at all launching areas or in nearby towns.

Note: Use map of entire islands.

TENT ISLAND: Perhaps this island could more realistically be described as a long point of Kuper Island's south end, almost equidistant from Crofton's Osborn Bay, and Chemainus' Hospital Point, bordered by Houstoun Passage and Stuart Channel. It lies in a salmon migratory route which would include Porlier Pass, and is thus a more constant producer than much of the rest of this three-island area.

Location: Approximately three miles from Chemainus and Crofton, six to seven from Ladysmith and Maple Bay. There are services available for boats, some bait and supplies and good anchorage and marina in Telegraph Harbour, where there is a passage between Thetis and Kuper Islands which is navigable at higher tides for shallow draft cruisers.

Where to fish: Most of the effort is at the westerly side of Tent Island and around into Houstoun Passage, according to the flow of the tide. There is a lighted rock (North Reef) one-quarter mile from shore which has the effect of creating a pocket of fairly deep (200 feet) water at this point and provides a clear trolling area.

Gear: More trolling is done in these waters than any other type of fishing, more likely due to the large areas which harbour fish than to their susceptibility to casting and mooching equipment.

Heavy to medium gear is used, with some downriggers and lift-off or release-weight effort. All light gear will work on the immature fish (bluebacks), and the outlook is fair for cast bait and jig-type lures.

Note: The channels get choppy according to the direction of the winds, but most of the area is safe for 14-feet and larger craft. Winds rise during the day, drop off at sunset.

KUPER AND HUDSON ISLANDS: Directly out from Telegraph Harbour on Kuper Island are three more islands. The southerly one, Hudson, is more associated with Kuper Island, having a marker light on a reef off its southern tip. Lying next to the indent of Telegraph Harbour, it possibly benefits from the general holding pattern of such bays. Locally, it is considered to be almost as good as the tip of Tent Island for spring and winter fishing, fair at all seasons for cohos with some chinooks.

Where to fish: The end closest to the passage into Telegraph Harbour, and out to the marker on North Reef. The tides are moderate.

Gear: More a trolling area than anything else, with inner shallows for light gear and casting.

THETIS ISLAND: Closest, at the north end, to Yellow Point at the Trincomali and Stuart Channels apex. An underwater reef, which is the continuation of the Island, has shallows which tend to hold chinook grilse and bluebacks in winter and spring, the best areas on the inner faces of Ragged and Miami Islets.

Where to fish: All the waters between here and Yellow Point have trolling possibilities all year, with August and September fair for cohos.

Gear: Because of the variable depths, this area is more of a light-to-medium weight gear fishery. There is some strip-, bait-, and lure-casting when the salmon move in.

YELLOW POINT: Yellow Point lies in almost a direct line from Porlier Pass across the end of Thetis Island and is considered a natural route for salmon returning to the Fraser River along the coastline by way of Dodd Narrows. It is also in the natural route of salmonids from the nearby Nanaimo River system. A popular nearby resort long ago established the presence of good quality blueback and coho fishing, and a fair number of immature chinook salmon during winter and spring.

Location: About three miles from Ladysmith, ten from downtown Nanaimo, it has its own ramp or can be reached from Nanaimo or Ladysmith launchings. Services are in both locations.

Where to fish: There is a fair tidal flow past the Point from Dodd Narrows and up Stuart Channel. The beach shelves out for some distance with depths of 60 to 240 feet. Along the drop-off on both sides of the Point and across the narrowed passage to the tip of Miami Islet is a pattern for trolling. Inshore the waters are fair to strip-, bait-, lure-casting and light trolling.

Gear: A medium-to-light-tackle type of water, with deep troll as an alternative. Since it is not a mature, big-fish area, mooching gear, light rods and reel are adequate.

Nanaimo is Vancouver Island's second largest city. As the center of a major sports fishing area, it has all services for visiting anglers.

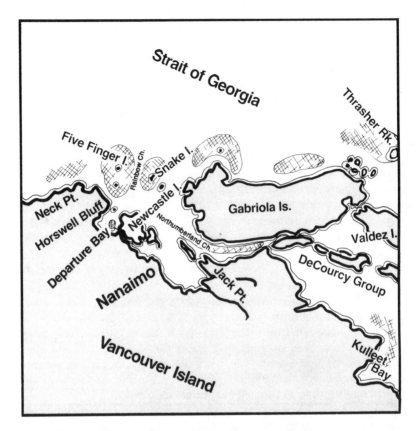

Rainbow Channel
Five Finger Island
Snake Island

Departure Bay
Northumberland Channel

RAINBOW CHANNEL AND VICINITY: On the seaward approach to Departure Bay the low-lying rocks of Snake and Five Finger Island and Hudson Rocks form an outpost bulwark of reefs that, in the fog, make Nanaimo an illogical deep-sea port, but an excellent fishing area. These offshore pinnacles have shallows and deeps around them which provide some of the most lucrative commercial and sports-fishing catches of salmon that originate in both the Nanaimo and Fraser River systems and, latterly, migrants from the Qualicum River hatchery.

The area has one of the most heavily fished coho-blueback populations of the inside passage, plus the immature chinook which begin in November and last through to June when the incoming mature chinooks for both large river systems move past these rocks.

Location: In a two and one-half- to three-mile circuit from Departure Bay entrance and Brechin Point ramp, or about five miles from Nanaimo's

Inner Harbour. All sources of fuel, food, bait, tackle, marinas, yacht clubs and accommodations are available at Nanaimo, a major city with a population of some 50,000.

HUDSON ROCKS: The first rocky islands visible after passing Horswell Rock light, and the next marker out to sea in almost a direct line to Five Finger Island. The rock and marker are both visible from shoreline.

Where to fish: Some anglers begin trolling in Horswell Channel at the first outward-bound marker, and move in a circle about the first group. The perimeter of the rocks is extensive, almost one-half a mile of shallows. A depth-finder is a great aid as there is no surface indication of the rocks. Once out of Departure Bay, the Red Can Buoy is an indication of where to begin fishing.

The outward side has 90- to 120-feet-deep water and is favored for trolling. Some strip-casting bait, or lure-casting is done, but there are no real holding places.

Gear: See composite at chapter ending.

FIVE FINGER ISLAND: Most often, when you ask a Nanaimo angler where he took his salmon he will tell you, "Oh, around the Fingers." His reference is, of course, to Five Finger Island, which is the western outpost of the ridge continuation from Hudson Rocks into mid-Georgia Strait. Five Finger is a flat, sandstone island which is a sea-bird habitat with the pungent stench of guano blowing off it during spells of warm days and light winds. From here outward-bound, the next stop is the Mainland.

Where to fish: Most angling is done in a circuitous route about the Island, which inshore has an almost due north and south oblong shallows to 20 feet, but which drops right down to 140 feet then to 180 or 240 feet, which is ideal for trolling any gear.

Strip-casting and jigging-type casting are done but not heavily pursued. The areas most open to Georgia Strait are most heavily fished and are sometimes more productive. Deep trolling with a downrigger is becoming more popular, using a pattern which takes the course of the commercial craft along the outer shelf of 480 to 600 feet.

Gear: See composite at chapter ending.

SNAKE ISLAND: Near due east of Five Finger Island lies the flat hummock of Snake Island. As indicated by the bulk of the island, and the light which is almost one mile distant, there is a large underwater shoal. The depths are 30 to 80 feet over much of it, almost at sea-level inshore, and tough to troll without a depth-finder. Trolling can be accomplished by staying at least one-quarter mile offshore.

Location: These are the next southeast reef islands showing after leaving Five Finger Island, the one in the direct line of the ferry passage to the Mainland. They are out in Georgia Strait between Rainbow and Fairway Channels.

Where to fish: The outward face seems to be favored with anglers who know the underwater contours. Or, using a depth-finder, take varied paths in a circuitous route around the entire Island. It is open Georgia Strait water with the offering of anchorage for strip-casting and lure-casting. There is seldom stationary mooching but some drift mooching. The south end Bell Buoy and the kelp beds are the best coho areas.

Gear for Rainbow Channel: Most of these island and reef areas are in the direct path of all Georgia Strait salmon migrations. In addition there are some underwater channels and reefs which are conducive to holding small feed fishes, and are a fair habitat for coarse fish such as rockfish and lingcod. Grilse can be found at all times. This means the smolts, blueback cohos and immature chinooks stretch the Nanaimo sport fishing possibilities to a full year-round fishery. Bluebacks are best in April and May, chinook all year round, either in the immature form or as returning migrants. Thus any tackle is useable, from the lightest strip- or lure-casting rods to the ever-increasing downrigger, all depending on the season. When cohos or bluebacks are around, small lures — flashtails, bucktails, hoochies, spoons, wobblers, anything bright and moving — with or without a dodger (but best with), also strip, bait, live herring or needlefish. Use red lures in early fishing.

Note: This area is prone to both southeasters and westerlies of rising and violent nature. If it is coming on strong, get out! Winds are usually minimal at dawn and at sundown.

DEPARTURE BAY: This once productive winter chinook water, one of the finest of the smaller, enclosed harbours on the coast, has been badly depleted with the loss of herring stocks in the area, but occasional salmon are still taken. It is sheltered behind Newcastle Island and the bulk of Nanaimo City. On the westerly shore the elaborate Federal Fisheries Biological Station nestles behind the reefs of Brandon Island, and to the south is the narrow waterway of Newcastle Island Channel. It is mainly a winter mooching area.

Location: The Bay is the B.C. Ferries terminal from Horseshoe Bay on the Mainland and is some 200 yards north of the Brechin Point public launching ramp, which is broad with a good number of trailer bays.

Where to fish: When the sometimes abundant herring run (that is before the intensive commercial roe fishery) moves into Newcastle Island Channel in mid-winter, and until it leaves, the chinook lie in the first deep (100-foot) water around Pimbury Point, which has the oil dock. Between there and Shaft Point shoal, where the water shallows for some distance out, and almost over to the ferry facilities, chinooks in their immature phase are in comparative ratio to the herring run. When the herring are in they can be jigged right in the fishing ground, or in the channel.

None of the rest of the bay equals this area. Further away from it the fishing becomes less productive. Also, it is not a productive coho fishing area.

Gear: This is a moocher's location of the same type as Horseshoe Bay's "Hole-in-the-Wall," subject to the same winter weather without the big Squamish wind; or, like Indian Islands in Pender Harbour, breezy but not dangerous to even the smallest craft — providing it is well handled.

Although some anglers troll in circles about the hole, it is perfect for one and one-half-ounce weights, on 9- to 11-feet mooching and stripping rods and reels. Not a bucktail-type area.

Note: Don't let your enthusiasm for a fish take you into the path of the huge ferries. BECAUSE OF THE CONFINED SPACE THEY COULDN'T GIVE YOU THE RIGHT OF WAY IF THEY WANTED TO. STAY AWAY FROM THEIR PATH!

NORTHUMBERLAND CHANNEL: The channel between Vancouver Island and Gabriola Island is just off the estuary of the Nanaimo River, bounded by Jack Point on the west and Descanso Bay on the east, then to the barely navigable channel of False Narrows and the fearsomely narrow and fast slit which is Dodd Narrows. Central waters are up to 390 feet, gradually tapering to 80 to 180 feet inshore, deeper and steeper on the Gabriola side.

Centrally on the Vancouver Island side, the smoke of the Harmac pulpmill marks the area individually, and the stench of sulphite on the water level as well as pulp manufacturing effluent is noticeable. Nanaimo River brings the salmon to the area, and it can be a chinook area at any time of the year, cohos lesser at any season. Immature chinook hang in the entire pocket, migratory chinooks moving in as they go up river. Don't waste a full day here.

Location: Almost due east, about two miles from the public Brechin Point launching slip using Newcastle Island passage out through Nanaimo Harbour. Nanaimo has all the amenities of a larger city — fuel, floats, provisions, bait, anchorage and wharfage (both at some premium in season).

Newcastle Island is a Marine Park which has several hundred feet of floats, mooring buoys, campsites, washrooms and other facilities, including 12 miles of trails for exercise. It also has a water-taxi service across to Nanaimo.

Where to fish: All the way from Jack Point up to the Percy Anchorage entrance to False Narrows, and back along the Gabriola coastline to Descanso Bay. Jack Point area no longer yields as many chinooks as it used to, but is an occasional producer. The whole booming area along the Gabriola shore covers a fairly narrow shelf almost, and even over, the drop-off. Fishing in close to the logs on a motor-mooch, troll, or drift-mooching and strip-casting works.

Gear: The whole area can be trolled with medium-weighted tackle, or anything from two ounces and dodger, to deep-planer or downrigger, as the bottom is virtually clear of reefs.

The season is short, with some winter and chinook mooching or trolling, then later in the summer and fall, to coincide with the salmon runs into the Nanaimo River. Bait is as effective as any gear, with light tackle for mooching-stripping. There is little, if any, light bucktailing.

Note: Don't attempt Dodd Narrows without 15 to 20 knots speed and a dependable boat, except at slack tide.

Chapter 4

SOUTHEAST COAST OF VANCOUVER ISLAND
Northwest Bay to Campbell River

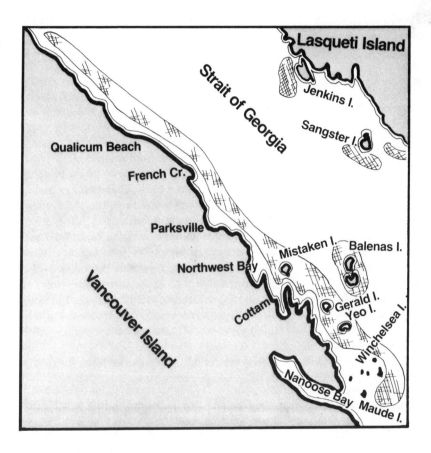

Northwest Bay	**Gerald Island**
Mistaken Island	**Winchelsea Islands**
Cottam Reef	**Jenkins Island**

NORTHWEST BAY: It is the main harbour between Parksville and Nanoose Bay, with a very bad exposure to westerly winds. In the inner portion, where Beachcomber Marina has a breakwater and float, ramp and dock, there is rental wharfage and some safe lee. On the opposite face, and in the end of the bay, booming grounds take up most of the shoreline.

Location: On a cut-off road into Nanoose Bay about four miles off the main Island Highway, the road divides. One branch leads to Northwest Bay and out to the tip of Cottam Point. The other goes in the opposite direction to the tip of Richard Point on the northeast exposure of Nanoose Harbour. A substantial marina, boat rentals, store services and accommodation is established at Schooner Cove. It is on the outside, the entrance to Nanoose (Bay) Harbour. On the road to Cottam Point, in Northwest Bay, the Beachcomber Marina has more facilities for services on the water. Both marinas have excellent launching ramps.

Where to fish: The actual inner bay holds immature chinooks from November until June, then some adults as they pass through. When the weather is calm, it can be fished even in a small boat by launching at the marina. Chinooks lie underneath the booms when the feed (herring spawners) are in, and can be jigged simply by dropping a line down with Buzz-Bomb or Silda-type lures from the outer logs. Some years this method provides phenomenal fishing. Trolling out to Mistaken Island along both shores and at mid-bay will also produce chinooks, both winter and summer.

Gear: Either deep troll, or light casting gear for jigging-type lures. Bluebacks occasionally move in, but are usually outside the bay.

MISTAKEN ISLAND: Off the end of Cottam Point, the peninsula which forms Northwest Bay, this rocky little island is one of the best year-round fishin' holes in a very productive area. It faces full into Georgia Strait, but is just enough offshore to produce a good passage between it and the nearby point.

All of its corners, or faces, have good fishing according to the run of the tide and the time of the year. Its little bay on the Northwest Bay side is a marker for anglers to turn by, its outer corner a point around which to work. The face along the opposite side is a catch basin for feed, and is often marked by early splashing cohos. Seabirds constantly wheel; cormorants and seals sit at rest on the westerly tip.

Location: A few hundred yards off Cottam Point, about one-half mile from the harbour of Northwest Bay and Beachcomber Marina which offers launching ramp and rental boats, gear and gas.

Where to fish: There is no consistently hot spot at Mistaken Island. It can be on either end or along either face. It is so small that half an hour of slow trolling will easily circle it twice.

During the winter, chinooks lie in the pass between it and Cottam Point and along its inner face. Since there are depths to 300 feet (120 in the immediate pass) and out to the point, they can be taken there all summer and into late fall as well. There are, however, fewer of them off the outer end and face.

Blueback cohos will often thresh on the surface on either side during the spring as they work the herring or other feed, more so on the inner face. When concentrated they can even be taken with a cast fly. They will also pick up any moving lure. Off the point the tides are fairly fast and trolling, casting, or drift-mooching are productive.

The area across the passage to Cottam Point, and down the shoreline, will also have this same type of concentration in early spring and summer. As the bluebacks develop into larger cohos, they are less thickly schooled and will move along most of the shoreline, but less in the passage.

Gear: This is ideal light-gear water as the feed is usually less than 25 feet deep in early spring and summer, and no more than 50 feet later. Any method will produce: strip-casting, drift-mooching, bucktailing, dodger and small lure, bait or jigging-type lures.

When the fish are further from shore they are deeper and a heavy troll such as downrigger or slip-weight will take them. Watch for the reefs off the outer and inner points which will snag tackle.

Note: Try all around the Island.

COTTAM REEF (Spar Buoy): This reef, with its visible spar buoy, is directly out from a former boat rental and trailer site called Claytons where a ramp still exists. It is the outer underwater peninsula which forms the very productive blueback nursery for which the whole area is well known. Most anglers use it as a marker, with Mistaken Island as the opposite end of an oval trolling pattern. The reef is the actual end of Dorcas Point which faces well out into the Ballenas Channel portion of Georgia Strait.

Location: Almost midway between Mistaken and Gerald Islands, one mile from Beachcomber Marina in Northwest Bay.

Where to fish: Taking the inner face of the bay between Dorcas and Nankivell Points as a line, stay inside the bay with the exception of a small passage about halfway from Dorcas Point, then out around the buoy in a semi-circle without getting too close if you don't know the water, as the unseen reef will snag any gear. When you know the passage, it can be safely trolled.

Or, use the buoy as an end marker, and fish the water all the way to Mistaken Island as a pattern for both trolling or casting. Like all reefs it has feed in close, and can be successfully strip, bait or lure cast.

The pattern of bluebacks and cohos is similar to that of Mistaken Island. If the fish aren't at one location they are often at the other, or in the open waters between and further out toward Ballenas Islands.

Gear: Light gear is excellent for most of this area as the fish are more in the immature stage (spring to early summer), leaving for their respective rivers in September-October, and are generally on the feed at some time of the day. Early morning has the edge for activity, but any time of the day can and will produce. When the bluebacks are on shrimp feed they are deep, and a deep troll used for chinook salmon will hook them, but it is not recommended.

Heavy gear is used by experienced anglers — dodger, planer, downrigger, lift-off weight, slip weight and release-weight — with any type of lure producing. Something with red, pink or orange (spoon, wobbler, fly, plug) in the one- to two-inch size is best in the April-June phase, larger lures later.

Parksville is typical of smaller communities which front the Strait of Georgia and supply a wide variety of angler services.

Casting gear provides the best sport, as the fish are not often large, not even the chinooks.

Note: The area is subject to very heavy winds which will spoil a whole week of effort. Morning and evening are the natural periods of calm when small boats are okay.

GERALD ISLAND: About midway between Schooner Cove Marina and Gerald Island is the largest of the group of islands on the way out to Ballenas Islands. It, and the surrounding rocks and reefs, are in the central area of some of the finest, almost year-round blueback-to-coho fishing on the entire inland passage.

Beginning in April, the bluebacks from the Squamish, Fraser, Nanaimo and Qualicum River systems intermingle in this productive salmon nursery area, and are nurtured by the herring spawnings which have been drastically overfished in Northwest and Nanoose Bays. Immature chinook salmon also abound in the waters, with a migratory route right through these reefs usually rich in feed such as jack-herring, shrimp and needlefish.

Location: Approximately a mile southeast around Dorcas Point, two miles from the inner harbour of Northwest Bay around either Cottam Point or Mistaken Island. All services, including a private ramp, gas, provisions, tackle, a little wharfage (very bad westerlies funnel into this bay) and guiding are at Beachcomber Marina.

Where To Fish: Off Gerald Island eastward toward Yeo Islands there is a rock called Douglas Island which has a deep face outward toward Georgia Strait. This Island is the centre of the group on an underwater reef which connects all of them to form a shallow in the 90- to 120-feet depths, ideal for holding feed and salmon. There are a fair number of rockfish, lingcod and other coarse fish, while needlefish and herring can be raked. This feed attracts the salmon and makes the early morning and low tide fishery an active one.

Salmon are taken to within 50 feet of the rock, all the way along the face, and past its outward point. Then move outward to an unmarked reef which is not seen at any tide but which lies about 600 yards northeast, and rises to within 15 feet of the surface. It is also very productive of salmon. The passage between Gerald Island and the shoals off Dorcas Point is a popular trolling area, producing either or both cohos and chinooks during most of the year.

Gear: It is a usual medium-to-light-weight tackle area, as is most of Georgia Strait, with downriggers and drop-off tackle used further offshore where commercial boats catch most of the chinook salmon during open season.

Any of the area will produce on flyrod and bucktail, jigging-type lures, even sinking flyline and streamer fly (silver or gold body), or small spinners and wobblers. Strip-casting, motor-mooching, drift-mooching are also productive. Some local boats carry long herring rakes to take jack-herring, or needlefish, which are most effective as bait.

Note: Both southeasters and westerlies will raise high seas in these areas and spoil fishing for days. Mornings and late afternoons are usually calmer.

YEO ISLANDS: This outer group of rock islands is about the terminus of angling originating from Northwest Bay. They are well into Georgia Strait, hence exposed to all salmon migrations up and down the coast, as well as to wind and weather. This is the real beginning of the concentrations of early bluebacks and springs, with good fishing continuing all summer and fall.

Location: About three miles east from Northwest Bay, past the larger Gerald and Amelia Islands, and out into Georgia Strait. Nearest land is Nankivell Point which has a marker almost midway. Services are at Northwest Bay and Lantzville from where Yeo Islands are also fished.

Where to fish: The outward face, in the direction of Georgia Strait, is popular trolling water. At the westerly end the reefs are close to the surface, and will snag tackle, but they provide excellent lure-, strip-, or bait-casting waters and light bucktailing. Cohos will be at all perimeters of these rocks, then move off with the tide and weather. Chinooks are taken on the inner, deeper channel and out to sea in the Ballenas Channel.

Gear: As for Gerald Island, anything from light to heavy tackle. An angler familiar with the area can do well with either.

BALLENAS ISLANDS: These islands are about one-third of the way across Georgia Strait from Vancouver Island. They are forested rocks with a prominent lighthouse at the westerly end which is visible to boaters in the main Strait of Georgia. Their inshore sides form the wall of Ballenas Channel, offshore of Northwest Bay.

The next nearest land across the Strait is the end of Sangster Island, with both locations in the migratory routes of salmon up and down the inner passage. As do all major reefs, these islands have a holding pattern for feed fish, plus sports and coarse fish. The major fishery is in summer as the passage to any near harbour can be rough. But chinooks do come from there in winter and spring, as they do all during the season. Cohos are around the islands, from small grilse through bluebacks to resident mature fish, and some of the big northern coho pass by.

Location: Nearly five miles from inner Northwest Bay, but actually as close as Yeo Islands, using Northwest Bay. Beyond the lighthouse there are no facilities. Remember that the area is open to very heavy winds and seas.

Where to fish: The lighthouse end has good fishing for cohos with bait or cast lures in the bay with the buoy, then outward toward Sangster Island, and down that side, off the far corner, and back up the inner side. The pass between the two islands is navigable in a small boat and has a bay with a steep northern face which holds cohos in all stages, some chinooks and coarse fish. This bay gives some lee in a southeaster, but fish move in and out of it without much of a holding pattern.

The bay on the opposite side of the pass has similar fishing characteristics, both being excellent for cast jig-type drift-mooching and strip-casting. Trolling is more general from the lighthouse side down to the southwestern corner. Covering the whole area provides a full day of fishing.

Gear: With more water to cover, and lots of depth, the area is more trolled than any other method, light-to-medium rods and reels being more predominant than heavy gear. Northwest Bay anglers, who fish it regularly, use jigging-type lures very effectively for both chinooks and cohos. Chinooks are taken almost any season. Any of the tackle normally used in the inland passage areas will work, with the stronger tides making mooching less productive.

Note: IT IS A LONG RUN TO ANY OTHER LEE IN A WIND.

WINCHELSEA ISLANDS (Grey Rocks): Usually described as "Fishin' at Grey Rocks" by far-roving Nanaimo anglers, the outer group of small islands is off the entrance to the big flats of Nanoose Bay, north of Willis Point and Maude Island light. It is a favorite fishing area for Lantzville and Schooner Cove Marina, but too far for most anglers from Northwest Bay. These rocks and reefs form the outer perimeter of the pocket of shallow water which attracts the fish. For this reason it makes the whole area one of the most intensively fished of the inland passage by both sportsmen and commercial fishermen. Being in open Georgia Strait, it has stiff southeasters and westerlies and is often unfishable.

Location: The closest access is from Lantzville, two miles, and Schooner Cove Marina where all services are nearby. It is also accessible from Northwest Bay, four miles from Schooner Cove or Nanoose Bay where there is a marina and ramp.

Where to fish: Grey and Rudder Rocks are the first reefs west of the

Navy marker on Maude Island, the down-strait end from Northwest Bay. They are the beginning of a pocket of shallows both toward Northwest Bay and behind Winchelsea Islands. Reefs abound inshore of these rocks and make deep trolling a hazard, but in a semi-circle outside of them trolling results are good.

Gear: All of these waters are light tackle, strip-, bait- or lure-casting (see Gerald and Yeo Islands).

Note: Leave quickly on a rising wind! It's a long way home either way.

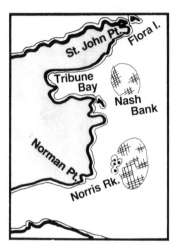

Norris Rocks
Nash Bank
Norman Point
Flora Islet

NORRIS ROCKS: These avian islands at the southwesterly tip of Hornby Island are at the entrance to Lambert Channel between Denman and Hornby Islands. They are the visible evidence of the shallow shoal which provides excellent fishing in this area.

The outward rock is an interesting breccia conglomerate where seagulls nest and continuously wheel overhead. The inner side, where many other shore and sea birds congregate, is a haven for often as many as two dozen colorful harlequin ducks. It is a low-lying island with bleached drift logs lying over it, a natural place for an experienced angler to choose.

Location: Although it is a common destination for anglers from Courtenay-Comox, it is more commonly reached from the nearer accesses of Bowser and Deep Bay or from the launching points on two of the largest coastal islands, Hornby and Denman. Both have good harbours, launching ramps, provisions, fishing tackle and some accommodation. In addition, there is a large camping, trailer-camp and launching ramp complex called Costa Lota south of Bowser for launching boats. The run is approximately five miles on open water. The Boyle Point Lighthouse on the tip of Denman can be kept on the port quarter for the approach.

Where to fish: During the summer there will be no doubt as to the locale of fishing. Boats from all over the area focus on the southwestern corner of the outer larger rock. There, a shelf with about 40 to 60 feet of water curves shoreward, extending to St. John Point on the eastern tip of Hornby.

The area is quite sheltered from anything but a southeaster, and is ideal for drift-fishing. The curve, both inward and outward, about 100 to 400 yards off the low-lying island favoring the Georgia Strait side, has excellent salmon fishing, as do the entrances to most similar channels.

Gear: One of the most popular methods of salmon fishing at this point is jig-type lure casting, mainly because the bottom is not over 60 feet below, the currents gentle and the water fairly calm. This condition allows the angler's craft to remain relatively stationary in order to work specific areas. Some strip-casting and mooching is done. Any rod from fly, light spinning to trolling will do since probably two-thirds of the effort is expended trolling. There is a channel in toward Hornby which is a portion of the troller's route.

Note: Subject to full force southeasters. If one is on the rise, the run back to Bowser and south is rough. Get out early at such times. There is a harbour close by inside the Lambert Channel on Hornby Island. Be prepared to spend a day in the area with this harbour as a refuge if required.

NASH BANK: If results aren't spectacular at Norris Rocks, the easterly mid-island waters by the Nash Bank spar buoy can be productive, particularly during coho season. This area lies off Dunlop Point on Hornby Island, the westerly corner of Tribune Bay. As there is no large rock island showing at this point, the locator is the spar buoy.

Location: About one mile from Norris Rocks which is the key position of reference.

Where to fish: The ledge which begins at Norman Point runs under the surface at similar depths, 30 to 90 feet. Anglers who know the location of the underwater troughs anchor or drift and run back to chosen positions, and use the lure-casting methods. However, most sports fishing craft circle, using a kidney-shaped pattern, the inner curve being toward Nash Bank, and the eastern end one-third of the way into the bay. The bay itself is sometimes productive for chinooks.

Gear: This bank lends itself more to trolling because the location of the holes where salmon can usually be expected is not exact. However, light gear is highly useable, while trolling with downrigger, planer or drop-off weights can produce good results. Bucktailing is always a treat since the waters are essentially shallow and conducive to holding feed. Some anglers work the points and kelp effectively for needlefish bait, the herring rake being a common piece of gear on local boats.

Note: All information applicable to Norris Rocks applies to this area. Leave a little more time to run for it in rising winds.

NORMAN POINT: This is the inside southwestern tip of Hornby Island on the run toward the ferry landing from Norris Rocks. It is a fairly sheltered stretch of water, less subject to the winds affecting the outer reefs, but more subject to a westerly pouring down open Lambert Channel from Georgia

Since the Strait of Georgia is part of the Marine Highway north to Yukon and Alaska, anglers can meet traffic from majestic ocean liners to booms of logs. Above is a deluxe floating sports fishing camp being towed to one of B.C.'s coastal inlets where 50-pound salmon are common and over 80-pounders have been caught.

Strait. Level beaches, ground to low spits by glacial erosion, give this area the look of a beachcomber's heaven. Although it is often neglected by anglers in favor of the outer face of Hornby Island, the stretch right up to the harbour from the channel between the outer rocks is productive of salmon, rockfish and lingcod.

Location: It is the southwest tip of Hornby Island with equivalents which apply to Norris Rocks. The ferry landing lies at the end of the stretch, and all amenities and supply items are available.

Where to fish: If the wind has risen too strongly to fish the more productive outer reefs, and often when the tide has turned to move the fish out of the latter area, this stretch along the beach and nearest to the channel opening between Norris Rocks and Denman Island is fairly productive.

Although the water deepens quite abruptly off the shoreline to 180 feet, there are pockets of kelp along the shoreline. If there are signs of herring spurting along the kelp line, a cast lure of the Buzz-Bomb or other types will bring results. More action seems to come from trolling in close. The better catches seem to favor the section nearest the channel between the reefs.

Gear: This stretch is probably more productive to trollers than casters, but any gear from light spinning and fly rod to heavy downrigger will take fish. Commercial boats ply this channel at specific times of the year, staying offshore. Planers, dodgers and all types of lures are effective, each in its season, with a tendency to pink or red earlier in the year. Bucktailing can be effective on surfacing schools.

Note: The ferry landing is nearby if it is necessary to sit out the weather. Most of the docks are taken up by residents and commercial fishermen during summer months. There is anchorage to the west. Watch for the reef at the harbour entrance. It can be a bottom basher.

FLORA ISLET (St. John Point): There are periods when the more open waters of adjacent Central Georgia Strait are favored, particularly the easterly point of Hornby Island. A continuation of the shelf making up the southern section of the Island, it eventually drops off into the 300- to 600-foot reaches of the Strait.

Probably the major runs of all salmon moving up Georgia Strait from the south, the natural runs of the Fraser River, and the northward-bound flow of the successful Qualicum Hatchery pass this corner, both leaving and returning. As does all the shelf, it has excellent groundfish and coarse fish production, and enjoys the passage of herring and other feed.

Location: The Islet is the point furthest east from the Vancouver Island shoreline, in a natural cruising line from Lasqueti Island which is also occasionally fished by craft launching at Bowser or Deep Bay ramps. It is the extension of a trolling line beginning at Norris Rocks. All facility and provision factors are the same as for the area.

Where to fish: The point of the Islet has shallow reefs, extending out for one-half mile, with depths to 180 feet. Any of this water will produce salmon and, if a line is dropped to bottom, kelp greenling, lingcod, rockfish and sea bass. The inner point is favored, and is productive during westerly winds; the outer Georgia Strait waters are favored near the turn of the tide.

Around Flora Islet, and between it and St. John Point, the waters are shallow and, unless after cohos perhaps seen feeding in the kelp, it is less productive than the outer perimeters. Some anglers troll the area toward Lasqueti Island for greater distances, a section favored by commercial boats. Inward of the point, toward Tribune Bay, the deeper waters hold chinooks.

Centrally on the point, and 100 to 400 yards offshore, the waters are less than 100 feet deep and tend to promote a jigging-type lure or strip-casting type of angling.

Gear: Anything from the lightest flyrod for trolling bucktail flies during the influx of cohos, to the deep troll afforded by the downrigger type of gear is used. Spinning type, or level wind casting rods and reels equal anything else when the salmon concentrate here. The effective Buzz-Bombs were developed in these waters, and they, with other jigging-type lures or trolled plugs, work very well. Bait is used in trolling, the planer type of sinker giving good depth control, with downriggers being more popular in the outer areas where the water is deeper.

Note: If the fish aren't biting at the westerly end, this region is the alternative. It is subject to the full force of a southeaster but is still protected from the westerlies. However, leave if the wind rises — and earlier than if fishing the inside point.

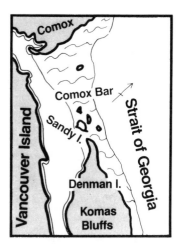

Komas Bluffs
Collishaw Point
Comox Bar (Inner Buoy)
Comox Bar (East)

KOMAS BLUFFS: About three-quarters of the distance northward along the Georgia Strait side of Denman Island the land rises in 200- to 300-foot bluffs of sand which are sometimes locally called the "Sand Cliffs." The cliffs are apparent from mid-Georgia Strait just after passing the northerly end of Hornby Island. They are not really an area that one would, from the general appearance of the surroundings, choose as the logical place to find salmon.

Yet here, too, there is an underwater geographical formation which provides a shallows before a deep. It is really the continuation of the lengthy Comox Bar. It connects Denman Island to Cape Lazo, having waters barely 24 feet deep, dropping off very quickly to 60 then 180 feet — enough to make it a fishin' hole. The sand cliffs themselves are not too common on the glacial terrain of Vancouver Island.

Location: Just about eight to ten miles from anywhere in this Vancouver Island sector if one takes the point of entry to the water. Occasionally used as a substitute for the fairly crowded fishing conditions caused by craft plying the Comox Bar Bell Buoy, it is also reached from launching at Deep Bay by way of Boyle Point and up Lambert Channel. However, a short ferry ride, often busy in summer, from Base Flat above Fanny Bay on Vancouver Island connects to Denman Island.

A four-mile drive across Denman takes you to Fillongley Park, a free and fairly small government campsite of rudimentary type and some beauty; then a further five miles southward is the ferry terminus at Shingle Spit on Hornby Island. There is an unused ferry landing slip beside the new ferry dock which has moderately good concrete launching facilities going well down to low water. The approach is precipitous, but useable.

This ramp lies approximately five miles south into the narrow channel from the best fishing areas. Both Islands have some facilities for boating, a few shops and about what can be expected for a rural area in any part of the continent. Summer visitors not numerous, probably because the Islands are somewhat isolated.

Where to fish: Favoring the area north of the sand cliffs at the end of the Island, and down past the higher cliffs reaching toward Lambert Channel, the whole area can and does produce both excellent chinook and coho salmon fishing in season. Because of its remoteness from most easy launching points, it is less competitive than Cape Lazo, Comox Bar or Norris Rocks, and it is more commonly trolled than any other method. If a concentration of small boats is moving around in the area, it's a good indication that they have located where the salmon are feeding. Keeping close to the drop-off along the whole stretch can also produce fish, using strip-casting and jigging-type lures.

Gear: While trolling gear is more commonly used, light tackle, particularly for bucktailing, can be excellent. In addition, the common jig- or bait-casting rods and reels are used. Currents are fair, as the area leads to the narrows of Lambert Channel. The shelf depths remain at an almost constant 60 to 120 feet, and that is where most of the inshore sports-caught salmon are taken. Such depths will handle a downrigger, larger planers and dodgers with heavy weight.

Note: Remember, any wind that is rising from the direction of your approach can mean a tough trip home. The best nearby harbour is at the Hornby Island ferry terminus.

COLLISHAW POINT: If you are heading northward up Georgia Strait favoring the Vancouver Island side, after passing Lasqueti Island the next island is Hornby, with Collishaw Point the first lee your craft will come into if you have a southeaster on your tail. It is a favorite long run for Comox-Courtenay anglers, the next stop onward from the sand cliffs (Komas Bluffs). The end of Hornby Island is comparatively low, with a long reach of shallow waters, plus a sizeable "cabbage patch" of glacial boulders which mark it from a distance. It is favored for coho and rightly so with its shallow seas over an extensive shelf. In fact, most of the travel of salmon up and down Georgia Strait is past this point.

Location: The northwestern tip of Hornby Island, a bit closer to the Deep Bay launching sites than from Courtenay-Comox. It is somewhat closer via the Lambert Channel ferry launching slip on either Denman or Hornby Islands. For amenities and services, see Komas Bluffs section.

Where to fish: The land projects along a low beach for one-half a mile in a triangle up the Strait, then tapers off on both sides of Hornby Island. At one mile from shore the waters are still only 30 or 40 feet deep, then they drop gradually to 60 to 120 feet. Although there is lots of water to fish, the tip to the Georgia Strait side is favored, as well as just inside the hook formed by the underwater reef.

Bait moves across this shallower stretch of water and the cohos move into the kelp, as well as over most of the shallows. Chinooks are taken in the area near the drop-off, with the outer tip of the point most fished. If a line is kept out all the way from this point to Floral Islet, at the other end of Hornby, it will be in fishing water which will produce at any time of the year, especially in summer.

Gear: Local anglers, who know how to line up the points, anchor on the drop-offs, using Buzz-Bombs or other casting gear. The waters lend themselves to any kind of fishing equipment from the lighter to the heavier type spinning, bucktailing, planers and downrigger (watch the abrupt inshore shelves with the latter).

It isn't the best area for mooching, because of its open large expanses and lack of easily defined holes, but drifting a 20- to 60-foot deep bait can bring fish. Here, too, local anglers take advantage of the abundance of bait and carry their own herring rakes. No question about it — fresh jack-herring or needlefish, so obtained, will catch more fish than any other lure, but any of the artificials can and will produce most of the time.

Note: Don't get too close to the shore at the tip. It becomes shallow suddenly and extends for a long way. If there is a rising westerly, it is a good time to leave.

COMOX BAR — INNER BUOY: After leaving inner Comox Harbour and the sandy point, there is a long stretch of open water to the southeast which is called Baynes Sound. It separates the mainland of Vancouver Island from Denman Island, and centrally averages 90 to 150 feet. About two-thirds of the way to the visible sandy islands at the beginning of Denman Island there is a passage across the shallows known as Comox Bar.

The first marker outward-bound is the conical red buoy which lines up with the Bell Buoy on the other side of the bars. It is an excellent fishing spot, particularly for chinooks, also some cohos and bottom fish.

Location: About two miles from the nearest launching ramp of inner Comox Harbour. Information on gear and facilities is the same as for the better known local Bell Buoy fishing area — see Comox Bar (East) which follows.

Where to fish: The inner side of the bar, about 100 yards off the Buoy and favoring the southerly direction, forms a hook. Depths rapidly drop to 90 or 120 feet. Depending on the tide and time of the year, this underwater bay holds chinook up to 60 pounds.

It is an excellent place to anchor and cast jigging-type lures for the chinooks. As the currents are moderate, the waters also lend themselves to mooching. If an angler follows the shelf, trolling can bring excellent results.

Gear: Local sportsmen favor this area as the best probable place to take a big chinook using a cast lure such as the Buzz-Bomb or Silda-type because it is less open to the heavier winds, yet is in the normal path of salmon moving into the river and crossing the bar. In addition, small feed also move over the shallows and from the kelp.

Not too subject to tides, it can be successfully cast on a slow drift, but anchoring and hanging off the bar over the drop-off allows the use of jigs, strip-casting or bait-fishing gear. Boats follow the long ledge, trolling with anything from light bucktail outfits to planers and downriggers. Once some of the most fabulous Tyee chinook catches on the coast existed in the estuaries of the Puntledge and Tsolum Rivers, but this sport has diminished with the loss of local runs.

Note: When the weather at the Bell Buoy is unpleasant, it is a good place to try on the way home or to pause at if outward bound.

COMOX BAR (EAST), RED BELL BUOY: The run from Comox Harbour's public launching and trailer parking lot is past the rock rip-rap finger, then a sandbar point to open water. The northern tip of Denman Island appears over the Bar, which shows that it is connected to the land mass of Cape Lazo. It is, in fact, an extension of it. The Bar has a varying depth of 12 to 24 feet over its four-mile length and forms a separation from Georgia Strait which it divides as a border of Baynes Sound. Almost open sea extends east from here to Texada Island.

Location: Pass the can buoy at the edge of the Bar, outward bound from Comox, the waters average about 12 feet for about three-quarters of a mile. Centrally lined up with the red conical can buoy is a spar-marker which is parallel in a line with the first marker, then to the outward Red Bell Buoy. The waters on the Strait side of the Bell Buoy deepen immediately to 50 to 150 feet and then to 120 to 240 feet.

Comox has a centrally-located marina, a three-car-width launching ramp, dozens of trailer and vehicle parking spaces, charging minimally for the service. On the main street there is a well-stocked sporting goods store, and on the lower highway, a bait shop. Since Comox is a sports and commercial fishing oriented community, there are charter boats, hotels and all necessary services for the visiting angler, with or without his own boat.

The harbour is good, quiet and has some anchorage near the wharfs, which is usually monopolized by commercial craft.

Where to fish: Immediately past the large Bell Buoy the water rapidly deepens. There is a slight channel inward bound, but it shallows very quickly. The waters within 200 yards of the marker hold a larger concentration of sports anglers because they gather there to Buzz-Bomb, a very popular local method. Some of the craft anchor; others who know the Bar well drift and run back occasionally.

A depth sounder is an ideal method of learning bar and positions, although charts show the curvature of its contour in a cup shape toward Cape Lazo which is the land almost due west. This stretch drops off sharply from 18 to 150 feet, and holds chinooks, cohos and pinks, as well as some bottom fish. Follow the drop-off of the Bar in either direction toward Denman or Lazo, and fishing results are good during the summer months. Such bars always have concentrations of feed moving across them, which seems to bring the predator fish.

Gear: Light gear is just as useful as heavier trolling gear, and during the late coho season a fast-trolled bucktail fly will produce excellent sport. Because Buzz-Bombs came from this area, heavy jigging-type lures such as Stingsilda, Strikers, Reef Raiders and others are popular, encouraging use of spinning and bait-casting rods. Indeed, a spinning rod of any kind is good tackle. At times, when the salmon are in the nearby kelp, they can be taken with a cast fly. There is always the hoped-for challenge of a very large spring, 30 to 50 pounds, taking the fly.

Trolling is the general sport, and anything from a downrigger, planer, or weighted lines with dodger brings fish. Cohos are often in the 50-feet depth by the Bar, or under the feed where they can be cast to with jig, or by strip-casting bait. Many local anglers carry herring rakes with them, some of the best being made by old craftsmen of the area.

Any lure from spoons to fly, jig, bait or plug will take both chinooks and cohos here. The proximity to the passage of salmon from the Qualicum River and southern-based hatcheries has kept the fishing fair, but the loss of the Puntledge and Tsolum River salmonids during the past 30 years has dropped the fishing far below its former levels.

Note: Early morning and late afternoon calms are normally the best water. A thermal wind which arises before noon and lasts until evening is common. If a southeaster wind develops get off the Bar. It gets rough.

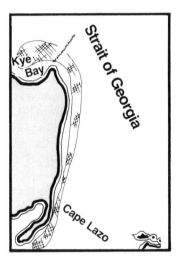

Cape Lazo
King Coho

CAPE LAZO: This Cape forms a major hook into the waters of Georgia Strait, an ideal habitat for feed fish, and a collector of salmon runs up and down that passage. It used to be noted for its Tyee salmon, the 30- to 60-pounders for which Campbell River is still famous. Just north of Comox-Courtenay, both favored as summering areas for tourists, it also forms the land protection for the largest Canadian air base and Kye Bay.

Location: It is the outer exposed point of underwater bars which stretch to sea for at least a mile in a sharp point. There is a private campsite with an excellent ramp near the point in Kye Bay up the coast, as well as the public launching ramp and facilities of Comox-Courtenay. A conical buoy in an almost directly northward course from the Comox Bell Buoy marks the inner shoal of 24 to 36 feet, and the beginning of the 42- to 120-feet line of the best fishing. If the Cape Lazo light is lined up almost east and west, the finger of shallows stretches about a mile into the Strait.

Where to fish: There is a pocket of 40- to 60-feet water between the Buoy outward toward Texada Island, then a return to 20 to 30 feet. All of this area of water is conducive to holding salmon and feed. The currents are stronger than in the waters off Comox Bar, and so is the wind, but the anchorage off these bars gives excellent opportunity to jig-cast, strip-cast, or drift-mooch.

When trolling a deep line the gear can snag on the bars, but a course southeast to Lasqueti Island will keep the craft in a good swing back and forth. Anglers who know the hot spots move in and out of them to give a fair indication of just where they are. It is a good idea for those unfamiliar with the area to follow their pattern.

This area, too, is on the migration route of chinooks, cohos and pinks in season. Fishing may be off one week and on the next, subject to wind and feed conditions. On the inside, there is some shelter from a westerly, or down-strait wind, which makes the fishing pleasant when other areas are enduring heavy swells.

Gear: This is strip-caster, jig-type lure water, just as is the inner bar. But, if you take cognizance of the number of commercial craft trolling the outer Strait, you will realize that a downrigger or deeply-trolled gear will take fish off the drop-off. It lines up with the Cape and inner side of Hornby Island, and drops from 120 to 240 feet then down to 420.

For the inner reaches of the bar, any type of spinning or casting gear is excellent, the same tackle as used for steelhead — a medium-to-heavy thread-line reel, or a level-wind for jigging or strip-casting.

Tides are fairly strong, but mooching is possible on any open reef or waters. Trolling with planer, downrigger (watch the sudden shoals), buck-tailing in season, plugs, spinners, spoons, bait — drifted or mooched — and herring in any type of use is productive. Bait can be raked in the kelp, a method locals use very successfully.

Note: The weather can build up fast, with the region open to a full southeaster. Watch the tides when returning to the beach ramps.

KING COHO AND VICINITY: Between Cape Lazo and the entrance to Discovery Passage, near Campbell River, the 30-mile-long shoreline is one continuous fishin' hole. King Coho is the site of a launching ramp and trailer camp of that name, one of several areas where boats and sports-fishing facilities are available. Right off the beach, during some evenings and tides, there are knots of surf-casters who regularly take salmon. One such angler won a Victoria-based derby with a 35-pounder one year. The beach slope is almost continuously gentle, with few indentations of the coastline between Cape Lazo and Campbell River. It is all salmon fishing water.

Location: The point of launching, King Coho, is two miles off main Highway 19, reached by somewhat zigzagging roads either from Courtenay or Comox, the latter being closer. It has both a rail-launched rental boat service and a launching ramp. All localized types of fishing gear are available, and some boat services. Closest general store is about a mile away.

Where to fish: Most of the fishing craft using the ramp confine their efforts to "out front," which means roughly three miles south toward Cape Lazo and 10 miles north toward Miracle Beach.

About one-quarter mile offshore the water reaches a consistent 30- to 120-feet depth, conducive to salmon passage and providing excellent trolling areas. It is, however, not typical of an area in which particular points can be designated as good mooching or casting places.

A few hundred yards northwestward along the shoreline the hook of the ferry landing provides enough of an indentation to provide a shallow bay, which is commonly the concentration area for anglers. It can be more productive than the fully open water, and is where most of the effort for chinooks takes place.

Gear: As has been noted, there is a growing tendency during summer days to cast from the beach, or any promontory of the Vancouver Island coastline. Thus, spinning, level-wind reels, rods and gear are useful. Primarily, any gear which will handle 20-pound test line can be used. However, since trolling is the most probable method along the off-shore, a medium-to-heavyweight set of gear is preferable.

Bucktailing can be productive when the salmon are feeding on the surface during any season of the year, but is predominantly used from July to October. Dodger and fly, spoon, strip, spinner, or hoochie are the usual lures, but planer with any lure, as well as the downrigger type of gear, are common and productive.

Note: The fishing can be excellent one moment, but quickly spoiled by winds. There is no protection from the full force of either prevailing southeasters or westerlies. Thermal winds can localize, to provide weather too rough to fish, while only 20 or 30 miles up or down Island the seas are calm.

GRANT REEFS: Along the inner coastline there are several reefs with fishing holes which the angler can pass over, completely unaware that they provide some of the most productive fishing. Grant Reefs is one such area. Others are Bjerre Shoals and Acland Reef a few miles further south.

In the full flow of the tides of the inland passage of Georgia Strait, these reefs are protected by their comparative remoteness from shore and their submarine invisibility. There is a buoy marking them to the south, difficult to pick up unless the navigator is on instruments. There are other slight signs, including a line of surface kelp which shows at passive tides and a scarcely apparent current slick, or disturbance which only a practiced eye might pick up. This is a really fishy area, as one cast, allowed to drop to bottom, will prove. Everything from a chinook to a sculpin is possible.

Location: South of the closest land, Savary Island, the reefs are a continuation of this land mass which includes Hernando Island to the north and

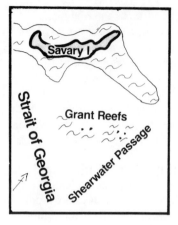

Grant Reefs

Harwood Island to the southeast. They lie about five miles out to sea from Savary Island, 15 miles north-northeast of Cape Lazo. Boats launch from Comox, King Coho, and as far north as Oyster River areas, which have full provisions, tackle and fuel facilities.

Where to fish: When the buoy is located, a semi-circle, bending to the south, keeps the angler on the main flow of Georgia Strait. Any northward transit moves into waters which are as shallow as 12 feet, seldom showing more than 30 feet, with one trough up to 80 feet. These shallows form a central point extending two miles in all directions — a confusing trait, unless equipped with a good chart or depth finder. The drop-off is gradual in a rough oval, pointed west. If the kelp is located there is scarcely a time when feed is not breaking the surface, or visible in the clear waters under the hull. When salmon are on the reef — between May and September, with chinooks longer — they break the surface near the kelp and jump on the outer perimeters.

Gear: It is ideal casting water for bait and lures of almost any kind. The shallows, and lack of surface indications of the depths, make trolling difficult, unless keeping a set distance to sea away from whatever may show on the surface. Anything that touches bottom is almost immediately grabbed by either immense rockfish, kelp greenlings, sculpins of the reef variety and, often enough, a chinook salmon. The salmon are often in less than 20 feet of water and can be cast for most successfully of all. Cohos move in among the kelp and can be fished almost like bass fishing, using a surface skipping plug when they are feeding. The use of an unweighted bucktail over the shallows is a method of trolling without losing tackle. Kelp does snag cast lures, but in its vicinity the chances of a salmon are better.

Note: The area is difficult to find because there is little evidence of it except for the buoy and kelp. Remember that unless the weather is forecast to be quiet and free of fog, it is a long way from shore in a single-engine craft. It requires from one-half to an hour to reach either shore under heavy wave conditions, and there is absolutely no protection from the full force of Georgia Strait's sometimes heavy weather.

Chapter 5

CENTRAL VANCOUVER ISLAND
Campbell River

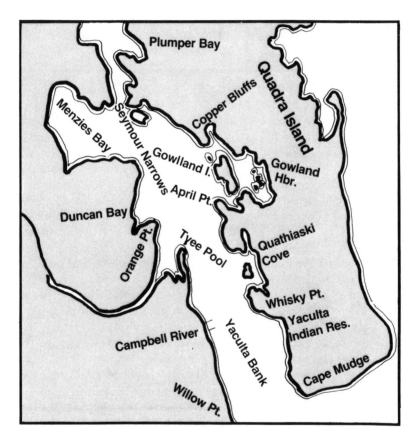

Campbell River

DISCOVERY PIER: Perhaps the newest innovation to B.C. anglers, this extremely well appointed fishing pier juts into the mainstream of the reversing heavy flow of tidal currents, indeed a departure from the past.

Entered from the main flow of traffic through the town of Campbell River, at the beginning of the main business area, the "L" shaped installation is available to the public for $1.00 a day, senior citizens free. It reaches out well into the main currents of these noted salmon fishing waters. Along its several hundred feet of railed-in pier, are bays and bait cutting tables, with strategically placed, glassed-in wind shelters as protection against the almost constant breezes (usually chilly) from the rapidly flowing tidal currents.

At the entrance is a convenience bar which offers light refreshments, with toilets nearby. At regular intervals on the dock there are large, light metal-ringed nets, complete with nylon rope for dropping down to the water (often up to 20 feet when the tide is out) and over which to slide the fish which has been played in from some distance. This netting is not easy for a lone angler, but usually other helpful anglers are nearby. The netted fish is then hauled up past the pilings to the deck of the pier. Nearby are fish cleaning tables equipped with running water and sinks, having convenient foot operated taps. (Just bring your own knife.)

The pier, which cost a million dollars, is extremely well planned and a favorite with anglers who have no boat. Because of the pier, they can say that they fished for salmon and coarse fish such as rockfish, lings, kelp greenling, etc. at the famed fishing Mecca, and perhaps bring home a salmon to prove it.

The first year's salmon catch was 150, with a 38-pounder recently taken. The pier will no doubt annually provide new local records.

Location: At downtown Campbell River on the Island Highway, just at the foot of the slight hill, the road to the pier entrance leads into a parking area which possibly will not be adequate during top seasons. The pier walkway leads out to the long leg in the turbulent green current.

Where to fish: There seems to be no early established, or specific pattern of catches, but the side facing the open water, and the pier ends, do regularly take fish. A line can be readily cast some distance out over the pier railings, using any weighted lure — Buzz-Bomb, Silda, Rip Tide, etc. — into regularly trolled waters. In fact, at the upward end of where the pier now sits, 47 years ago I caught a 37-pound spring salmon on a plug while in a rowboat, and several smaller ones and cohos since. Because the 37-pounder is still my largest after almost half a century of salmon fishing, I can vouch for the water's productivity.

For today's fishermen live bait is available at the nearby fish dock a short walk away and is commonly used. There are rod holders, actually prepared emplacements, cut into the railings to allow for a rod being left extended seaward. However, it would be unwise to leave gear unattended for long as it could tangle with those of other anglers downstream in the current. There is no reason why the inside portion of the pier would not be a temporary holding area for herring, thus an attraction for predatory fish such as salmon, lings, etc.

Possibly the main warning about fishing on the pier is to be very careful of the swing and direction of your cast so as not to harm or entangle neighbouring anglers.

Gear: It is entirely possible, although not too efficient, to cast out a hand line, or dangle it from the pier. The most logical gear is an 8- to 10-feet casting rod with either a spinning or level-wind reel. There is no reason, however, why the drum reel used in strip-casting methods will not work, except for the possible entanglement in feet (your own and others). Mainly used among artificial lures is the type known as "jig" which loosely includes Buzz-Bombs and Stingsilda-type weighted lures to provide a long cast and depth penetration. (Tidal flow is up to 13 knots.) Bait is used, live and strip, or plug cut. It isn't a place for a dodger or planer type, except perhaps at the pier ends, where it would flow in a straight line and not tangle with other gear. Check local customs and regulations before beginning angling.

Note: The pier is an excellent opportunity to watch others fishing, enjoy the view, or rest in the shelters and partake of the light refreshments at the entrance to the main section.

Cape Mudge
Light House

CAPE MUDGE LIGHTHOUSE: Starkly white lighthouse buildings mark the location of the point of Cape Mudge. Just a few hundred yards off these buildings, both inside the narrows and outside, the waters constitute one of the hottest sports fishing spots of the entire Pacific coastline, changeable in mood or success.

Approaching Campbell River from either the north or south, Quadra Island is the main shoreline directly across the waters of Discovery Passage. Cape Mudge is the southwestern tip of Quadra Island and its lighthouse a focal point for herring to mill on the tide. Usually their presence is indicated by pitching and wheeling seagulls, the best sign of salmon below.

Summer coho fishing is superb, with a good sprinkling of chinook salmon. Lingcod, rockfish, sea bass and kelp greenlings abound at all seasons. (Try the greenling for culinary excellence!) Winter chinook salmon bucktailing can be extraordinary, with fish to 30 pounds.

Location: Almost equidistant from Campbell River proper and Willow Point, fishing is done mainly at the opposite ends of either side of a one and one-half mile triangle. Cape Mudge Light can be seen clearly from either location. Since there are no services of any kind, your boat should be provisioned and gassed-up for a full day BEFORE leaving.

The run across the narrows is a thriller to the novice, as the swirling currents throw even a fast boat around. While the combers of a tide rip can be both dangerous and menacing, they can be navigated in a boat as small as 12-feet, but 14-feet and up is recommended. Most boats travel across the passage from their launching on the opposite shoreline, a few coming from Quathiaski. There is no season in which fishing is totally non-productive. It is just more productive during selected months.

Where to fish: Tide currents swirl and eddy over the drop-off which quickly deepens to 70 feet, and inshore to the beginning of the kelp. Here salmon feed on needlefish, but they often extend across the entire channel, with the first 200 yards offshore being most popularly fished.

The edge of the drop-off, in water from 35 to 100 feet, is more productive of chinooks, but has prolific numbers of lingcod, rockfish and kelp greenling. The back-eddying current is excellent for dropping a winter bucktail. It is here the gulls usually wheel and dive for herring, the latter occasionally quite visible, flashing in the turbulence beneath. It is this turbulence which brings the bait fish to the surface.

As previously noted, salmon move on the tides, thus inside the point can be best at one time, outside better during the opposite flow. Salmon species (both cohos and chinooks, sometimes pinks) will on occasion be offshore as much as one-half mile. A good clue is to watch the movement of other fishing craft and their activity. Netted fish are quite easy to spot and men playing rods bent outward to stretched nylon is another good indicator.

Gear: Almost any known type of fishing gear is used here, from handlines to fly rod and reel. The same applies to lure and baits. The most continually successful summer season baits are herring, available at Quathiaski Cove, the Indian Reserve, and the Campbell River - Willow Point areas, and needlefish (generally taken with herring rakes by individual effort). Plugs, spoons, bucktails, flashtails and hoochies can be equally deadly some days. The use of Buzz-Bombs and other jigging-type lures such as Stingsilda in British Columbia had much of its early acceptance in these and nearby waters.

This is also the domain of the deep-troller, dodger-flasher, drop-off weight and downrigger. Commercial boats sweep in close, and it is wise to keep out of their way. Medium-to-light rods will give the most sport, but can be broken by salmon which have been recorded up to 70 pounds in the nearby Tyee Salmon Club records.

Note: This area shelves very quickly into shallows as land is approached. Deep tackle is often lost. Approach to Cape Mudge is perilous for any foolhardy or incapable navigator. The currents are fast, up to 12 knots. The wind builds up fast, and a small boat should stay away if whitecaps are visible. Many 12-feet ones go across, but 14-feet is a safer minimum.

WILLOW POINT: Mention the name Willow Point almost anywhere anglers gather from British Columbia to Baja California, and someone will

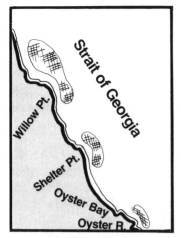

Willow Point

step forward and begin to relate the size and extent of his catches. The area enjoys the largest summer population of non-resident anglers of possibly any place in Canada.

The reason is very simple. It is one of the best all-year-round fishing areas in the world. More particularly, it is a salmon angler's Mecca. And, if salmon is too rich for your menu, it is almost impossible to keep lingcod, rockfish and bottom fish off your hook.

Location: Approximately a mile south of the main business section, hotels and commerce of Campbell River, the major up-Island community with a population of 17,000. There are hotels, campsites, restaurants, grocery stores, tackle shops and boat rentals on both sides of Highway 19 which runs along the beach. The ramps are good, the fees reasonable, the boat rentals normally-priced.

Where to fish: A few pulls on the oars will bring the craft out to the edge of the kelp bed, which stretches almost continuously along this shelving shoreline. Depending on the time of tide and year, this beach-front water can be successfully fished using a fly outfit for cohos and some grilse and casting outward to the edge of the kelp.

Beyond the string of black-brown bulbs and their hanging ribbons, the serious fishing begins. The sudden drop-off in the clear waters is visible to the eye. Along this underwater shelf the chinook salmon lie, up to 100 feet deep. During winter and some evenings, however, bucktailing in as little as 20 feet of water proves successful.

Cohos, too, feed along the kelp, chasing the jack-herring and needlefish. They can be trolled, cast to with jig-type lures, bucktailed, spin-fished, mooched or strip-cast. They will, at times, take any lure from fly to plug, or live or cut herring, and so will the chinook salmon. Cohos can at times be taken in all waters between Willow Point and Cape Mudge, often seen breaking on fry or jack-herring in the slick turbulence from the nearby Strait. Commercial craft work the deeper, offshore waters. Anglers using downriggers can get the same results.

Campbell River's million dollar fishing pier is the first on Canada's Pacific Coast. The 600-feet-long pier, complete with rod holders and fish cleaning tables, juts into some of the most productive salmon water in the area, yielding chinooks 38 pounds and over.

Gear: Any type of fishing outfit has taken salmon off Willow Point, but a medium trolling rod, reel, dodger and lure is the predominant method. Bass rigs are capable of handling fish, as is fly gear, but spinning gear with longer, 8- to 10-feet rods and casting plugs are more productive.

The epitome of all small (up to 40 pounds) game-fish angling is reached by the motor-mooching method, using a large bucktail, three-eighths ounce of bead-chain weight, salmon fly-reel and light fly rod (graphite is superb). This technique is known as winter bucktailing, beginning in December and lasting until March. At this time the average catch is between 6 and 25 pounds, all immature chinooks.

Cohos are bucktailed without weight any time from March through October. Coarse fish, lings and rockfish, often take the salmon lures even in the shallow water, particularly chinook-type, polar bear hair flies. Trolled or mooched herring is also grabbed off quickly, although mooching is made difficult by the very strong currents.

Note: The tides emanating from Discovery Passage through nearby Seymour Narrows are world-feared by big ship operators, and have speeds up to 15 knots. The fresh winds moving up these straits can make a maelstrom out of these waters when combined with the normal twice a day tide rip. Small boat operators should make for cover on a rising breeze, with either side offering shelter. The bays of Quadra Island have both moorage and anchorage, but Campbell River has only jam-packed artificial moorage, little if any anchorage.

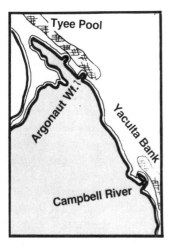

Campbell River Foreshores
Argonaut Wharf
Copper Cliffs (Bluffs)
April Point

CAMPBELL RIVER FORESHORES: Just south of Campbell River there is a knob of high land which separates the city from flatlands. There is a coastal indentation, not really a bay, near the beginning of Yuculta Bank, with a discernible contour. The bank itself is a jut of submarine land which extends halfway across the channel, averaging between 30 and 80 feet in depth, obviously a continuity of the hummock of land ashore. This description will serve to denote boundaries for the area.

The turbulent shallows terminating or bordering most tidal rapids provide feeding and breeding grounds for many sea species. This particular area has produced some of the finest and largest salmon ever recorded, both cohos and chinooks. When the seaside town was a small village it was, with the Tyee Pool, the most consistently fished of local waters. The busy marine traffic discourages its modern use, but it is still very productive, although the angler may have to dodge a Quathiaski ferry while playing a salmon.

Location: The visible boundaries are the southern knob, or hill, and its coastal indentation. The northern terminus is the end of the tall buildings and business section — always plainly in view. All seaside amenities are near — wharves, breakwater, bait, boat gas, and across the main street, tackle, gear and groceries. Launching areas are close by in both directions.

Where to fish: Actually, if one does not withdraw the lines while fishing northward from Willow Point or southward from the Tyee Pool, the prospects of catching salmon (or coarse fish) are continuous. The back-eddying which occurs near the kelp beds at the foot of the bluff of the high land is a productive area. The edge of the kelp can be excellent for either casting, stripping or fly-casting for cohos.

Chinooks inhabit this area all year round, cohos from May to November. As in most narrows, runs of herring pass in and out on the tidal ebb and flow, and during their migrations. Because the whole narrows is a major trough to the outer ocean, pelagic fishes must pass through it, thus the angler has the possibility of catching not only resident fish, but also migrants. There is a back-eddying of currents behind the breakwater to the harbour which is productive, but the entire Yuculta Bank waters are shallow enough to be ever productive.

Gear: This area is subject to fast currents, running 8 to 11 knots, and has only short periods of essentially slack water. It is never actually free of roiling currents and its very slickness is mistakenly believed to be calm. Because of this turbulence, only the inshore back-eddies can be plumbed with lighter-weighted gear.

Generally, the waters require substantial weight to take a lure down. It means that medium-to-heavy-weight trolling gear — drop-off, ball weight, downrigger — is more consistently reliable for reaching the depths at which chinooks usually feed. Cohos can be taken on bucktails, but not as successfully as in the shallower, less continually turbulent reaches.

It isn't the ideal place for light tackle, but on occasion when the fish are feeding on the surface, catches are made by casting either lure or fly. Anchoring for strip-casting is difficult.

Note: A motor is a necessity unless the angler is a strong oarsman. As there is a lot of local boat traffic, including a regular ferry from the harbour, the angler must learn to give way to it. Don't fish there unless you know you can run back the one to three miles which the currents will carry you by the time you land a big chinook.

ARGONAUT WHARF LAUNCHING RAMP: Just north of Campbell River is the large Indian Reserve which occupies most of the land between Campbelton and the main township. This area consists of a delta strip pushed outward into the narrows by the accretion of silts and boulders on the south side of the river for which the area is named.

Along the nearly straight shoreline and before the more northerly and world-famed Tyee Pool which has attracted famous people from around the world, is a fishin' hole which offers some of the best northern district fishing. Like the adjacent stretch of water which passes the town, it holds a prospect of fish of all kinds: cohos, in their May to October season, and chinooks all year round.

Location: It is just over a mile from the town centre, with a public launching ramp on the famous Campbell River Tyee Spit. Beside the Spit is one of the busiest small seaplane bases on the continent. The Spit also offers a commercial campsite, most other boating necessities and, in season, a crowded non-resident population.

If you pushed your boat out by hand, and it caught the current, which it can barely escape, you could throw a line in immediately and have a fair chance of catching a salmon or some type of edible bottom fish. It is the most spacious place for launching and leaving a trailer, but very busy during most months, almost impossible without a wait during early dawn and sundown hours. It is at the northern end of Yuculta Bank, where the water deepens quickly to 180 feet.

Where to fish: There is a strip of shallows approximately 100 to 200 yards wide and 50 to 90 feet deep which holds chinooks and it is at a drop-off. Such areas usually attract both bait and game fish. As the waters are seldom without heavy currents, a motor is almost a necessity to keep any pattern of angling. This pattern should be inshore to within 50 yards in some places, 150 yards in others, particularly for chinooks, although the maturing cohos do move in. As is usual in all locations in this area, cohos will surface-feed well offshore and chinooks will also move out. During the last few minutes before darkness, however, both chinooks and cohos move to within a few feet of shore. The limits of the stretch go past the large pier to the south and, of course, infringe on the Tyee Pool to the north.

Gear: Strong currents preclude the results which light tackle will give in still waters, but they don't make it useless. Motor mooching with from 4 to 10 ounces of weight, downrigger and heavy trolling tackle produce excellently. Strip-casting and jigging type of fishing brings results right off the pier end, particularly during winter.

COPPER CLIFFS (BLUFFS): Copper Cliffs are noticeable on the Quadra Island shoreline even from Campbell River. Their sheer drop is green with moss and stained with the blue oxide of their copper rock content. In the fissures of the cliff face murres nest and paint white streaks down the steep sides to illuminate the greys and greens.

The Cliffs are part of the point which forms the northerly buttress of the big bay with Gowlland Island as its centre, then curves back to April Point. This proximity to the deterred flow of the tides from Discovery Passage provides a mixture of currents, and is in the path of migratory fish either way along the passage and out of the shallows of Gowlland Harbour.

Actually, the full force of tides flows along Copper Cliffs, the shoreline having depths of about 80 feet, dropping immediately to 180 feet. This area has always been a favorite for guides in the area, and has an abundance of salmon of both species during their seasonal runs, some chinooks in mid-winter, but better at the height of the migrations.

Location: It can be approached along the coastline from Quathiaski Cove, or included in a lengthy trolling section starting with the curve of April Point then somewhat northerly across the passage from Duncan Bay, where Orange Point is the closest land.

Most often anglers approach it from the Campbell River side, from a Spit launching, or river mouth harbourage. There are no facilities closer than Gowlland Harbour, Quathiaski Cove, or April Point.

Where to fish: Anywhere along the face of the green cliffs from the hook into May Island to the little bay northward will produce both cohos and chinooks in their season. The flow from Entrance Bank comes past the point, and in that area the tides are least strong.

Along the face the full force of Seymour Narrows moves, with the water shelving deeply. Perhaps the best results are from trolling, and that can be anything from a deeply-weighted line to a bucktail. If the cohos are showing on the surface, there is little chance of missing action. Chinooks are less likely to show and are taken deep and closer in to the shores. Needlefish, raked locally, are highly productive in the whole stretch.

Gear: Because of the predominantly strong currents, this is not a mooching, strip-casting type of water. Bucktailing, lightly-weighted needlefish, and jack-herring can be surface-trolled or cast, with a greater tendency to deeper trolling gear.

Note: This is fast water, deep and not too treacherous, but a boat with a motor should be used.

APRIL POINT: Almost directly across Seymour Narrows from Painter's Lodge lies April Point on Quadra Island, forming the hook of Gowlland Harbour into which Gowlland Island fits. In fact, from the Campbell River side it appears to be a single shoreline. April Point juts into the currents from the inward tidal flow and forms a back-eddy which is compounded by the flow of waters forced outward from Gowlland Harbour.

This confluence of almost constantly moving waters over fairly shallow depths of 50 to 100 feet in the pocket behind the point, and the shelter of Steep Island, tend to make it an extremely good habitat for all fish from herring and coarse fish to salmon which move in and out. The hole is scenic, sheltered from southeasters and highly productive of salmon, lings or rockfish.

Location: From the nearest point — Quathiaski Cove boat ramp and dock — it is one-half mile around the corner and up the Strait. From the big boat launching ramp at Tyee Spit on Vancouver Island it is one-half mile across the open waters of Discovery Passage.

Bait can be purchased at two outlets in Quathiaski Cove and, if the plant chooses to supply it out of season, from the processing cannery in the nearby cove. The village of Quathiaski Cove has most stores and amenities, plus a launching ramp beside the main docks. Gas and oil are available at the piers.

Where to fish: The natural contour of the area is immediately suggestive of where to concentrate. The hook of the point has a guest lodge and boats and a tall white flagpole. Steering a curving line from the point slightly inward toward the entrance of Gowlland Harbour, a near 90-degree turn at the first shoreward point of Gowlland Island, then along the kelp line up to the beach several hundred yards northward, will keep lines in continuously productive fishing water.

Circling the bay point to point, and outward past the point into the flow of the main current, will bring cohos and chinooks. The section of this curve inward to Gowlland Island is possibly the best chinook salmon sector all year round. Anywhere a baited line touches bottom, rockfish, lingcod and kelp greenling take it, and all these fish will also take deeply trolled flies and hoochies.

Gear: Since this water has a more gentle current than most shores because of its sheltering points and intervening islands, it is ideal for any tackle — mooching, trolling, strip-casting, threadline-casting and bucktailing. The flow of the tide is changeable, causing the bite to fluctuate. It is ideal early morning and late evening water for chinooks in winter. Anchoring is possible.

Note: When the wind blows you off Willow Point, Cape Mudge or the Campbell River shoreline, April Point offers shelter. The waters in the shoal between Gowlland Island and the mainland of Quadra Island, at the April Point entrance, are shallow and therefore hazardous at low tide or for the novice navigator, but they lead to protected waters.

QUATHIASKI COVE: This easterly terminus of the Campbell River ferry is a busy little pocket harbour with docks which jut right into the fishing waters. Quathiaski itself is a picturesque northern fishing village, visited by boats from all over the coast and well known to anglers. It has wharfage, boat ramp, stores, bait, gear and some inland accommodation. After a long run up Georgia Strait from the south, or northward from Seymour Narrows, the harbour and its calm bay are a welcome relief from hours at the wheel.

The bay is a haven for herring which attract the larger fish. Boaters often slip dinghies into the slick but restlessly moving waters which eddy from Discovery Passage through the northern and southern entrances, around Grouse Island and out. Occasionally, anglers reach their limit in an evening after supper, both on chinooks and cohos.

Location: It is the main port on Quadra Island. There are large wharves with the launching ramp near the ferry slip.

Where to fish: Both north and south entrances to the cove are on Dis-

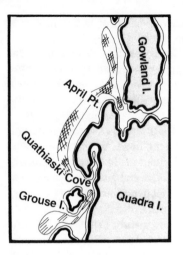

Quathiaski Cove
Whisky Point

covery Passage, and have eddying currents which attract and move salmon, herring and coarse fish about. Fishing can be productive in these entrances. The most successful effort is expended in the deeper waters off the southerly end of Grouse Island, which lies in mid-bay and is a buffer from the tides. It is excellent for cohos during their season from blueback to mature fish. Due to its fairly consistent depths of 50 to 90 feet, it also holds chinook, but ferry and boat traffic interfere with consistent fishing. In evening and early morning it is sometimes boiling with feed and salmon.

Gear: The confined nature of the small harbour of Quathiaski isn't suitable for broadly sweeping trolling rigs, but bucktails, lightly-weighted bait, mooching, and jig-type casting gear are all effective.

Note: Expect to give way to marine traffic. It is a busy harbour.

WHISKY POINT — CAPE MUDGE: This area is the long section of the shoreline of Quadra Island that stretches from Quathiaski Cove to the Cape Mudge Lighthouse. It forms a deep enough bay to provide some shelter from the full currents running in the main passage. A major and prosperous Indian Reserve and village occupy the shore and upland of the southwest portion of the Island.

Whisky Point is the land which forms the southerly point on the curve of Quathiaski Cove. It is fished in continuity after trolling out of the harbour. From its rocky bluffs, the indented coastline again curves eastward almost to the Indian Reserve, then outward to Cape Mudge.

Every section of these waters holds coarse fish and salmon at all times of the year. It is possibly one of the most productive and consistently fished stretches of water in the district.

Location: The northerly end is directly opposite the launching ramp at Tyee Spit, the southerly end almost directly across from the launching areas south of Campbell River. Quathiaski Cove facilities are closest with bait, gas, gear and most other essentials. Campbell River has all such services and much more, including a diversity of accommodation and food services.

Where to fish: Whisky Point at the northerly end is in the full flow of the Narrows and is heavily and productively fished according to the tide. The water deepens quickly from 60 to 270 feet and is extensively trolled. These depths taper off just past the point heading south over a ledge of 30 to 90 feet of water from the point to Cape Mudge. Along this drop-off there are favored spots of many anglers.

Just north of the Indian village of Cape Mudge the waters are more shallow all the way south to the lighthouse. Any of these waters, including all the way across the narrows, can produce chinooks and cohos, plus lots of coarse fish — lingcod, rockfish and kelp greenling. The more heavily fished and thus consistently productive area is the shelving off the coast between the Indian Reserve and the point.

Gear: This is a multi-tackle area, fly rod to downrigger. Because of the almost continually fast moving currents, heavily-weighted trolling gear predominates. However, the back-eddying current in the hook of the land north of the lighthouse produces excellent bucktail catches, both on summer and fall cohos, and on winter chinooks.

Possibly, medium to heavy trolling gear is best all-round, but in some portions of the shallows, casting and threadline gear using plugs and jigs produces. Strip-casting can work, but mooching bait is difficult.

Note: When the weather off Cape Mudge is too heavy for comfort there is little shelter in this stretch. Don't try to fish it unless you have an adequate boat for bad weather.

Wilby Shoals
Orange Point

WILBY SHOALS: Probably the most extensive fishin' hole on the coast, this area centres on the greatest flows of water in the Inland Passage and has some of the best all-year round fishing available anywhere. Specifically, it is one of the finest sports-caught, coho salmon producing grounds in the

The southern tip of Quadra Island with Cape Mudge Lighthouse near left center and Wilby Shoals, one of the world's most productive coho waters.

world. There is no portion of it, from nearly inshore against the sand cliffs, to two miles out, in which the angler cannot expect a strike, with chinooks in the deeper areas.

It is primarily a summer fishing area. The reason is that it is open to very stiff breezes, even gales, which blow counter to the strong tidal flows over shallow reefs, forming combers that will drown even a mid-size cruiser if caught at the wrong time. Wilby Shoals consists of the southeastern shallows forming the underwater tip of Quadra Island between the points known as Cape Mudge and Francisco Point. They form a triangle which reaches one and one-half miles into the top end of the Strait of Georgia, with depths varying from 20 to 50 feet, ideal nursery and feeding grounds for both salmon and coarse fish.

Directly in line with the inward flow of tides from Cape Mudge there is a reef averaging 20 feet with a fairly gentle drop-off to 80 feet.

Location: The area is that eastern bulwark off the southern end of Quadra Island which is visible on the highway approach to Campbell River. The closest Vancouver Island launching points are the beach ramps from the area between Willow Point and Campbell River. However, almost every boat launched in any area nearby ends up off Wilby Shoals at some time. It can be reached just as easily from Quathiaski Cove which lies to the north. Campbell River and the Willow Point area are the nearest sources of gear, supplies, bait and shelter.

Where to fish: Fishing is good over its entirety at times. Tidal flows, which are strong to medium, back-eddy and swirl across this underseas tableland. The bottom can be clearly seen over much of it, and is a good guide as to where the boat should be. If the bottom is clearly visible, it is an indication that the angler is in waters too shallow for larger salmon, but is likely to find a lot of immature salmon or grilse in the one-half- to two-pound size. When the bottom is obscured and the waters appear to be dark, the craft is in a better position for larger fish. Cohos abound across the entire reach during many days.

Some anglers prefer to follow the evident contour of the long finger of reef which extends in a direct line to the termination of the shoals from a point beginning at Cape Mudge Lighthouse. Commercial boats use this stretch as it is productive in the deeps and less liable to snag their heavily-weighted gear.

Almost in the centre there is a stretch of 30 to 50 feet of water which always seems to hold both feed and salmon from May to October. Cohos appear here as bluebacks, maturing to major trophies later in the year. The area toward Francisco Point along the flow of waters from Sutil Channel is also favored, but to a lesser degree than the areas closer to Cape Mudge.

Gear: As is the case with Willow Point and Campbell River, any type of gear has been proven successful in catching salmon, rockfish, sole, lingcod, kelp greenling and a myriad of other edible fish. It is a medium-to-light tackle area, in the sense that strip-casting, spinning, jig-type casting, bucktailing, (weightless for cohos and with minor weights for chinooks), trolling with lightly-weighted dodgers or flashers, mooching or drifting with live or cut bait will take fish. While it is a prime bucktail or light troll area, the outer edges of the shoal require heavy weights to get the lure to the proper depths.

Note: Don't stay out on Wilby Shoals if the weather is building up a wind. Don't go over there if whitecaps or combers are apparent. It is a dangerous shoal during such times, and should be avoided by boats having deep draft. Take lots of bait. It is a long way back if you run out. Remember also that tidal flows are noticably strong and will take a boat a long distance while a fish is being played.

ORANGE POINT: This area would be better described as a nondescript stretch of salt water border of beach and timber which separates the famous Tyee Pool and Duncan Bay. It is an interim phase in which boats from the Tyee Pool enter or travel to Duncan Bay, or vice versa. The angler is often surprised that he has a fish on during this traverse. It shouldn't be a surprise. The submarine hump in the coastline juts right into the main flow of the waters to and from Seymour Narrows. Inshore it has its own minute shelves and drop-off. Back-eddying occurs from the point which forms the cup of Duncan Bay, site of the big paper mill. Both chinook and cohos are taken along this stretch with a fair to good chance that a lingcod will grab the lure.

Location: Roughly, the coastline which lies along the Narrows from the mouth of the famed Campbell River itself, passing internationally-known Painter's Lodge and the Tyee Camp, up to the point which forms the entrance to Duncan Bay. Boats and services are available along the stretch, but the public ramp on nearby Campbell River Spit is the usual access point. Expert fishing and boat guides are available at the local services.

Where to fish: About midway from the Tyee Camp, or Painter's Lodge, there is an undersea jut of land which rises up in a shallows to form a slight bank and some turbulence. This is in proximity to the oil company wharf, and is holding water for both bait and salmon. Between the shelf and the point of Duncan Bay there is more likelihood of taking fish than anywhere else. Fast currents, up to 10 knots, move by this land and a boat should be equipped with a motor for trolling.

Gear: Because of the almost continual turbulence and fast currents, general usage is heavier trolling gear, but like most places in this extraordinary salmon fishing district, casting lures or baits can be successful. It isn't particularly good for mooched lures, but can be productive on bucktails when cohos are showing on the surface.

Note: Try it when nothing is showing either in Duncan Bay or the Tyee Pool. It often has chinook and some cohos moving through.

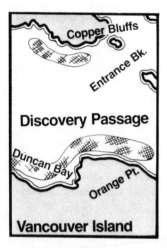

Duncan Bay

DUNCAN BAY: This Bay once had probably the largest pier-based salmon fishery in the world. On a hooked promontory, it juts into the full flow from nearby Seymour Narrows through which pass most of the migratory fish of the inner passage. Overshadowed by the enormous paper mill, with its dense, billowing, stench-filled clouds of steam, one would not expect it annually to produce as large a catch of sport-taken fish as almost any other bay. Stuffed with booms, buoys, chip scows, and pillared with pilings, it also has the white and brown frothy scum from wood pulp on the water. Only the continuous tidal flushings save it from complete pollution. Yet, it is a salmon rendezvous for both local residents and visitors, a definite contender for some of the larger catches of chinook, both in size and number.

Location: It is approximately two miles north of Campbell River along

Highway 19 to Sayward, or up Discovery Passage by craft toward Seymour Narrows. The paper mill, first visible at sea from the top end of Georgia Strait, or as a source of white steam from the city, uses the promontory forming the bay as its centre. There is a paved road leading right into the heart of the plant and onto private property. Permission to fish from the end of the pier can be requested. Plant employees fish from the dock with cast lures both during the day and under the brilliant nighttime lights, often making excellent catches of chinook all year round.

The public ramp at the Campbell River Spit is the usual access to the bay. The local marinas and stores in both towns have all supplies and accommodations necessary to anglers and boaters, although wharfage and anchorage are scarce.

Where to fish: As has been noted, resident anglers take salmon by casting from the piers. The front of the mill is probably as productive as any. Anywhere from the point inside the curve of the bay to the far end produces chinooks.

The bay is from 60 to 120 feet deep, and is occasionally still enough to mooch because the hook of the point creates back-eddying. It is out of the main force of the current, under the protection of the outward thrust caused by Race Rocks. Generally, a few to 200 yards off the pier heads, booms, and buoys is the path chosen by anglers. The section along the northerly booms is as good as any or out in the area where the water deepens over the edge of the shelf, although this position is subject to fast tides. Cohos sometimes break water to feed along this faster current.

Gear: This is a composite tackle area, with a leaning to medium-to-heavy, except for dockside casting, where steelhead, spinning, mooching and strip-casting gear is useable. This gear is also useable from a boat in the bay. Some bucktailing is done, both for cohos and winter chinooks.

Most generally, the area is fished by trolling with a motor, although it can be motor-mooched quite successfully. Plugs, spoons, dodgers, flashers and herring, whole or cut, are all good producers in this bay.

Note: Early morning and late evening is often the best time for Duncan Bay. Watch for tug and barge traffic and rising winds. It is a good run back to the Spit or river mouth.

MENZIES BAY: Seymour Narrows, one of the most swiftly-moving tidal rips in the world, flows and ebbs from Menzies Bay which forms a bowl for continually roiling waters. The big, spacious Bay is never at rest. Although from the shoreline it might appear slick, calm and silent, even at the largest ebb and flow it is deceptive. It has some of the most dangerous currents and fastest peripheral tides of any in the inland passage.

Because of its proximity to the 14-knot flow from Seymour Narrows, the angler should approach it with a boat not less than 12-feet. However, a 14-feet craft is recommended with a good motor capable of moving the craft at a speed of at least 13 knots to offset the tidal flow.

It is safe only along the Vancouver Island shore, and even there is not

Menzies Bay
Plumper Bay

recommended for rowing or canoeing. It is sheltered during a southeaster, and lined with mills and booms with good kelp beds off the southerly regions. And, it has some of the best salmon fishing waters adjacent to Vancouver Island. The rockfish, lingcod and sculpin populations are as numerous as anywhere, with chinooks all year round and cohos and bluebacks from March to October.

Location: About six miles north along Highway 19 from Campbell River to Sayward, the big Bay comes into view from the pavement. A series of logging and mill sites occupies the first portion of the southerly beach. Near the inner end a dirt road parallels the highway, having a none-too-clearly marked cut-off near a mill site. Follow it to a double fork in the road, then down a rutted road to a lightly bulldozed clearing, and an open space of gravel contoured roughly down the beach. A boat can be trailered to the water's edge at mid-tide, the beach being passable on good tires, but it is unsurfaced. Most boats run up from Campbell River launching or moorages.

There is no store, or any services or accommodations. Bring everything with you.

Where to fish: Menzies Bay is huge, adjacent to the shores of Quadra Island, Maud Island and Seymour Narrows itself. Thus, when an angler says he is fishing Menzies Bay, he may mean behind Maud Island, off Race Point, or behind Ripple Point. All of those areas produce chinooks and cohos in season. Dropping a line anywhere in the water and hitting bottom with jig or bait is almost sure to bring up fish.

Taking a line south of the launching ramp to the first two Vancouver Island bays, the lines of kelp bulbs will be noticeable when the current isn't too fast. Off these kelp beds, chinooks and cohos can be taken. In the central portion of the Bay, during a flowing tide, there will be a noticeable rip. Along its edge the salmon feed on the herring. Wheeling, pitching gulls are the best signs. Remember that the tides off Race Point run 10 knots and can be scary.

Gear: There is water and room to use any gear in Menzies Bay. In fact, chinooks are caught off the booms by casting lures. Mooching can be successful anywhere, with spoons, plugs and bucktails also used. Because the central part of the bay has water from 70 to 180 feet, trolling is productive with even the heaviest gear — downrigger, planer or drop-off weights. The shores shoal from 90 feet to 20, with Defender Shoal at mid-bay only 20 feet deep. It is along the external drop-off of this shoal that salmon are more likely to be taken, and any gear can be used.

The waters are always disturbed, which means that a well-weighted lure must be used to keep depth — and even that gear will be tossed around.

Note: Menzies Bay, inside of the hook of Race and Stephenson, or Wilfred, Point, is very deceptive water as the currents flatten it most of the time. The speed of the tide is phenomenal, the whirlpools and boils unnerving and very dangerous. A newcomer should not go outside mid-bay unless tides are at slack. And it is wise to be equipped with an auxiliary motor. There is inshore anchorage but no public wharfage.

PLUMPER BAY: Just through the worst portion of Seymour Narrows on the east side, a welcome bay perhaps one-half mile wide becomes evident. Like many such bays on this world-famous tidal flow from the Pacific, Plumper Bay has a continuously changing series of back-eddies with few still portions. Ringed with rock bluff and timbered shorelines, it has, at the inner curve, a fairly good beach, some safe anchorages and a couple of small homes. It is an excellent bay for cohos during the summer, fair for chinooks at any time.

Location: Across the channel from Menzies Bay about one mile by boat, it has no facilities. Access is either from the ramp at Menzies Bay or one of those at Campbell River or Quadra Island, possibly from Browns Bay which has a summer lodge. This Bay is directly across the swift waters of the channel, a somewhat scary crossing at any time, and most definitely not to be attempted in anything but a large boat capable of 20 knots and with an auxiliary motor.

Probably the best approach is to cross to the east coast from Menzies Bay, run up close to the bluffs and rocks and take advantage of the somewhat lesser turbulence along that edge. During full tides 20-feet-deep whirlpools develop without warning — AND THEY ARE DANGEROUS.

Where to fish: Only during the slack-water tide in Seymour Narrows are the points of the bay subdued enough to fish in any manner but trolling. The currents are so fast and variable that controlling the boat occupies one person almost completely. Experienced anglers who know the area even work in the faces of the Narrows.

On an outgoing tide, however, the southern end of the Bay offers immediate relief from faster waters. Trolling is done from this end of the circle to the northern extremity where, at the same tide, fast currents become too strong to keep a lightly-weighted lure down. Inward flowing tides to some degree reverse the areas of slacker water. Both points offer excellent coho fishing, the inner bay being more productive of chinooks but sometimes equally good for cohos. The entire Bay holds a good population of coarse fish — lings, rockfish and kelp greenlings. Herring can at times be jigged in the back-eddies.

Water depths are 48 to 120 feet in the inner section of the Bay, to 300 feet along the northern bluffs.

Gear: Because the Bay is subjected almost constantly to strong currents, trolling is generally productive, some heavily weighted, some with downriggers. Casting with lures for cohos can be productive but like most of the district the common lure is herring strip, plug, slab, or some needlefish. Plugs are effective, as are spoons.

Note: A boat smaller than 16 feet can be sucked easily into a whirlpool, with drownings not uncommon in the vicinity of Seymour Narrows. Don't go there if you panic or aren't a competent boatsman.

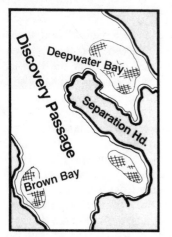

Deepwater Bay

DEEPWATER BAY: The next fairly secure bay in a line north from Plumper Bay is well-known Deepwater Bay, a very popular place with some Campbell River anglers, but not too well-known to visitors. Separation Head, a long finger of moderately-rising headland, disguises its presence until the boater moves out of Plumper Bay, and suddenly finds an almost duplicate bay. Being further out of the full flow of the turbulence of Seymour Narrows and facing into broader Discovery Passage, Deepwater Bay has continual but less turbulent currents and back eddies. The definite hook of the point to the south provides calmer waters and beaches on its inner circle, plus a long stretch of fairly deep water along the northerly side which is centrally marked by a logging installation.

Location: One-half mile north of Plumper Bay, with the same launching approaches and a scarcity of facilities for anglers or visiting craft.

Where to fish: Deepwater Bay is fished in almost the same manner as Plumper Bay south of it, anywhere from the point of Separation Head, where cohos often move about, to deeper into the shoreline. Here chinook are more inclined to take advantage of the moderating depth which is from 30 to 100

Campbell River calls itself the "Salmon Capital of the World." Among facilities are 12 resorts, over 20 hotels and motels, 16 RV Parks and Campgrounds, boat rentals and airline service. In summer marinas are crowded, although an $8 million complex which includes 1,200 marina berths will help when it opens in 1991.

feet. The shelf disappears at the northern slope of the Bay, giving way to waters which quickly drops to 240 feet just offshore.

Trolling is done all along the inner contour of the Bay, casting and mooching in the back-eddying portions nearer the point. Even the center of the Bay can produce salmon during most summer and autumn months. The area has a fair amount of feed, herring being jigged near the flow of the current. Like most such remote bays, it has an abundance of coarse fish — rockfish, lingcod and greenling, among others. Some clams can be found on the beach, as well as crabs in the shallow shelving inner reaches. Winter fishing is minimal.

Gear: More moderate currents allow a better probability for mooching and casting for salmon, but heavier trolling gear is more commonly used. The currents are fluctuating at all tides and fairly fast, thus lures such as plugs and spoons on deep lines are productive. Herring strip and locally raked needlefish are preferable, but when the cohos are breaking the surface anglers can use bucktails and unweighted gear with a good chance of limiting out. As in many such bays, its unknown quantity as to what will produce fish leaves lots of room for experiment. It is very likely that any lure at a given time will bring a limit as the Bay is a natural first catch-all for fish travelling this route to and from the open Pacific Ocean.

Note: Once again, it must be pointed out that the approach to this Bay is dangerous during flood tides, only slightly less so at slack water. Once reached, however, it is a moderately safe body of water.

Chapter 6

NORTHERN VANCOUVER ISLAND
Kelsey Bay to Beaver Harbour

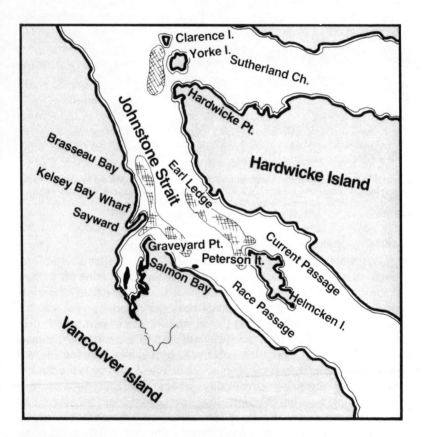

Kelsey Bay Government Wharf
Brasseau Bay   Hardwicke Island
Graveyard Point

KELSEY BAY GOVERNMENT WHARF: Although it is difficult to say where in B.C. casting a lure for blueback coho began in earnest, the government wharf at Kelsey Bay is now one of the prime locations on the coast. Sometimes, with positions to cast from the tall, creosoted pilings at the end of the wharf at a premium, there will be 10 to 15 anglers on the decking. And, there's great excitement when one of them hooks a chinook to 20 pounds. But, immature salmon do gather behind the hook of the rocky point and feed in the crystal clear waters formed by the back-eddy of the fairly fast-flowing tides. Often beginning in December and following through until April, the bluebacks move and the anglers with them.

Location: At the end of the road which leads onto the wharf, one-half mile past the village of Sayward.

Where to fish: The tall pilings of the wharf offer height from which to cast, most fishing done with jigging-type lures, on some days the color determining the catch. While the central part of the wharf gives more room to play the fish, at times either corner will be closest to the salmon. Some anglers climb around the rocky coastline to the north of the wharf and cast from the rocks, with equal success. Landing from the wharf is traditionally done with a net on the end of a long line, the tired fish slid into the ring, then hauled to the decking. Some small boats move into this area of fishing, both trolling and casting.

Gear: The prevalent methods are the jig-type which can be tossed a long distance, thus covering more and deeper water. Any cast type of lure, however, has a good chance.

KELSEY BAY: Limiting the boundaries of Kelsey Bay to the area between the northwesterly point and the land just past the delta at Graveyard Point offers one of the major fishing places in the area. The chart shows no particular name for the point itself, but its steep, rockbound face has a patch of kelp in the tidal eddy, and the fishing begins there.

Behind the tall pilings of the government wharf is the small, public, fish boat harbour tucked against the rip-rap. Just beside the wharf there is a good, private launching ramp but it has the worst possible curve in it, particularly if the driver is an amateur.

Fishing begins in mid-winter and drops off with the movement of the bluebacks to Campbell River or northward during May, then improves from June to September and slows in October. Once the site of the finest salmon and steelhead runs on the Coast, hydro development in the watershed, coupled with intensive and almost century-old logging and commercial fishing, has depleted the localized Salmon River run.

Location: The community is spread over a distance of some eight miles between Sayward, which is a coastal settlement over 100 years old, and the harbour which is Kelsey Bay. The areas have gas, oil, food, lodging, some guiding, tackle, bait and, as mentioned, a launching ramp at the side of the government wharf. Actual tie-up room is at a premium during the summer because many commercial boats use it as a base. There is nothing that could be considered safe anchorage.

Where to fish: A line can be trailed astern outward from the ramp and be into a salmon before the pier end, but the westerly point gives excellent water depths, dropping off to 180 feet almost immediately. Retracing the course southeasterly along the front of the dock and former ferry landing, then along the front of the booming grounds and river mouth to Graveyard Point puts fishing gear in productive water during the whole length. This pattern is the general beat of the trollers, then outward into mid-Strait, according to the tide and wind.

Near the first point a cast line, bait and jig-type lures will take fish, as will trolling, the former being more productive.

Gear: This is an all-type gear area, according to the section chosen. Spinning, casting, fly rods, even the lightest, will take bluebacks and smaller chinook. Bucktailing is possible any time.

Trolling gear, from downrigger to planer with dodger, is the popular method with anything from cut-plug to fly, or salmon plug. Two ounces and dodger works well on cohos, as does drift-mooched herring strip. The tides are fairly strong, but back-eddies allow gear to go down. Not really a moocher's prime area, but feasible.

Note: It is extremely difficult on a westerly wind; bad enough on a southeaster. The tide kicks up haystacks off the points and river mouth. Don't try it in a small (12-feet) boat unless it is fairly calm.

BRASSEAU BAY: Just over one-half mile northwesterly up the waters of Johnstone Strait after leaving the point of Kelsey Bay, this little bay curves deep enough into the high bluffs of the timbered coastline to provide a private little harbour. Its point is not named on the charts. Kelp beds patch the shoreline all the way, with a large bed to the Kelsey Bay side and a small

Although southern Vancouver Island waters receive the most fishing pressure, anglers are venturing to other parts of the Island. Port Hardy, some 300 miles north of Victoria at the end of pavement, is hosting increasing numbers of visiting and resident anglers.

patch off the other end of Brasseau Bay. These continue around the point into a lesser bay a distance of less than one-quarter of a mile. All of it is salmon water, and will produce rockfish and lings, but it drops off very quickly to 180 feet.

Location: It is the first bay up Johnstone Strait on the same side as Kelsey Bay.

Where to fish: From the kelp patch on the inward side, right into the bay, then around the point into the next bay and point (unnamed) there are excellent back-eddies which hold feed fish and salmon slashing on them. All of this is a productive lure-casting, drift-mooching and strip-casting area, despite the sudden drop-off into the deep water. A lure, cast inward from a trolling craft, anywhere, will produce cohos at all ages, smaller grilse during summer seasons, and chinooks when they are moving through.

Following the indentations of the bays from the point, as close as 30 feet from the kelp, will pick up coho on bucktails or on two ounces and dodger. A few feet further out, the deepest of trolls brings up chinook salmon at almost any time of the year, the Tyees in August and September, although off the river mouth is the popular area.

Gear: (See under Kelsey Bay.) Drift-mooching and light tackle are just as responsive.

Note: Tough to fish in any wind. Don't go out into these waters without a dependable motor, as the tides are up to five knots, and there is no shelter beyond the small inner bay.

GRAVEYARD POINT TO PETERSON ISLAND: This is the section of the Kelsey Bay area, deeper into Race Passage, which is named for the speed of the currents caused by the narrowing of Johnstone Strait between Vancouver Island and Helmcken Island. Major fishing craft ply the pass with nets and troll, but the inshore is specifically where sports anglers concentrate their efforts. Waters shallow around the reef where Peterson Light is the marker, and Hkusam Bay is the inward water.

Location: From Graveyard Point or Peterson Light it is about one mile to Kelsey Bay Harbour when heading inward on Johnstone Strait.

Where to fish: As in all narrowing passages where there is a race during one tide and a back-eddy on the opposite run, these waters are favored on the run outward. Inshore, there are shallows and reefs to 20 to 25 feet, which drop off quickly about 400 yards offshore. All the fishing area is lure, bait, drift-mooching and casting water, with trolling good on lightly-weighted gear, in fairly close. For heavy gear a line drawn well outside the marker of Peterson Light is advisable. As it is all under the influence of the freshwater flow of Salmon River, it is more or less as productive as the Kelsey Bay waters.

Gear: Specifically, the same as described under Kelsey Bay, but watch for shallowing ledges when using deep gear.

Note: Tides are too fast to row against. A good motor is a necessity. Don't head out here in a westerly wind.

HARDWICKE ISLAND (Earl Ledge): On a clear day, from the wharf at Kelsey Bay, there is a tiny settlement in view directly across the reach of Johnstone Strait just above where Helmcken Island splits the flow of waters. It is called Hardwicke Island, situated on the big island of the same name.

Out in front, Earl Ledge has its beacon marking the ridge of underwater land which forms the northerly end of Current Passage. This is the reef to which the Kelsey Bay-Sayward locals graduate when weather and time permit, and the season is compatible. From Hardwicke Point to the west there is shoal water from 60 to 180 feet, then around Earl Ledge it becomes quite shallow and is the passage for salmon migrations.

Location: Approximately one and one-half miles directly across Johnstone Strait, on the closer tip of Hardwicke Island.

Where to fish: From the little bight indented into the main Island, which forms the small harbour for the settlement, outward in a semi-circle down Current Passage and along the shoreline in a "U" to where it straightens out. The flow of the tide from the passage is up to five knots, forming a back-eddy on either side of the light and turbulence off the reefs.

Inshore of the very steep drop-off there is shallow water in a ridge which runs right into the harbour of the bay. All of this area around the marker is productive of cohos on light tackle, both cast and troll, and both hook-ups yield chinooks at most times of the year. Feed surfaces in the exposed kelp beds, and can be a sign of feeding salmon. Commercial trollers fish the central channel into Current Passage, and out into the center of Johnstone Strait. Care is needed with a deep troll on the approach to the light and for some distance around the perimeter since most of the water in close is from 60 to 120 feet with some exposed rocks. Trolling from this point across to nearby Helmcken Island, and down that coastline on either side, can be productive, also to the focal point of Yorke and Clarence Islands up the Strait.

Gear: Inshore it is a light tackle, casting bait or lure type of water; offshore, any type of tackle used commonly on the inside passage. Hoochies are good lures. When the sockeye salmon are in the area, they will take pink or red hoochie or squid-type lures on the deep troll. Bucktails, in all hues, will produce salmon.

Note: Mornings and evenings usually have calm waters and are prime times for salmon, with chinook close to the surface on coho gear at times. BUT WHEN THERE IS A WESTERLY WIND, IT RISES MID-DAY TO HEIGHTS WHICH BLOW UP WAVES DANGEROUS FOR SMALL BOATS.

It is popularly stated that southeasters don't affect the fishing conditions in the Kelsey Bar area, but that is not so. Don't cross the Strait in a small boat unless you are willing to stay on Hardwicke Island until the wind goes down. JOHNSTONE STRAIT HAS STRONG TIDES. WHEN RUNNING AGAINST THE WIND THE COMBERS ARE LARGE AND STRONGER THAN IN OPEN SEAS.

BEAVER COVE: This is a very large bay near the north end of Johnstone

Beaver Cove
Telegraph Cove

Strait, and used to be the terminus of the ferry run from Kelsey Bay. Now it is served by a road which is mainly paved and is essentially a center of logging operations. The excellent harbour, much of its shoreline occupied by log booms, includes the estuary of a good-sized steelhead and salmon river named the Kokish.

Several years ago accommodation for anglers and campers was leveled in the northwestern portion of the shoreline and a launching ramp installed. But in recent times the directional signs all indicate Telegraph Creek as the area for launching and camping.

A good mile deep, the bay itself offers lots of water to be explored. The river mouth obviously attracts salmonids into the bay. One regular angler proclaims that spring salmon fishing right off the booms is highly productive during the winter and spring months. During July and August there are good catches of chinooks, cohos and pinks. Black sea bass (a rockfish) are abundant in the daytime during mid-summer.

Location: Reached from the main Vancouver Island Highway at a well-marked intersection, approximately 130 miles from Campbell River, then along a paved road about nine miles, which ends in gravel and company roads. As it is a company-controlled area, most side roads lead to one of several logging operations, with the main offshoot going to nearby Telegraph Cove. There, all essential services are available.

Where to fish: As previously noted, this bay is broad and deep. Even the locals can't (or won't) be too specific. But, both the north and south points have the full race of the tide converging from Queen Charlotte and Johnstone Straits. There is a tendency to fish off the points, and across the width of the harbour mouths, trolling between the two headlands with some curvature inward into the bay itself.

Herring break the surface, almost like constantly-flowing water, in the nooks off these points. If a line gets to bottom with bait on it, rockfish, lingcod and, in particular, black sea bass take it almost immediately. Jigging herring is nearly impossible because the immature black sea bass grab the bait, every barb taken before the line can be dropped to any depths.

Gear: Most local anglers troll. The majority of them use heavy gear, up to two pounds of weight, a dodger and a lure. Frozen, cut herring is available at Port McNeill, 15 miles away, but bait seems to be grabbed immediately by the abundant coarse fish.

During the pink salmon runs, a red hoochie behind a dodger or a flasher is very productive. Fairly fast currents pass along the front of the harbour, swirling in back-eddies deep into the bay.

Note: A 14-feet or smaller is adequate for fishing this area, but tides are strong with winds heavy sometimes. The bay is an excellent harbour at its inner depths.

TELEGRAPH COVE: Telegraph Cove has become a major sport fishing area. As the surrounding land area is steep, and the harbour confined, the actual water frontage is jammed with service facilities. Included are a store and eating place, an extremely compact marina-wharfage which almost fills the end of the cove, and boat charters for fishing and whale-watching cruises. During the busy summer months it is difficult to find room to turn around near the main installations and there is little available parking.

While it is a rustic area, it is also picturesque and worth the drive in from the main highway if fishing is the objective. Facing on Johnstone Strait, the bay is small but fishable, major efforts being expended outside the cove. It is the next southerly bay along the coastline southward from Beaver Cove.

The main campsite is well past the immediate area of the bay and is where anglers park their trailers and vehicles. All major services such as food and fuel are available.

Location: Approximately two miles from the crossing of the Kokish River Bridge, along a gravel road which is also a mainline for logging operations, and which has several off-shoots to company sites. Distance from the Island Highway is about 10 miles. The next major source for all services is the town of Port McNeil, approximately 16 miles farther north along the main highway.

Where to fish: Many local anglers prefer the water lying to the south down Johnstone Strait to those adjacent to either Beaver or Telegraph Coves. There are 10 miles of fishable waters to comb before reaching the contour off the mouth of the Tsitika River. The whole stretch produces fish during June to September.

Although chinooks are taken right in the small harbour, most of the trolling is done between the point and into the bay behind the small islands. The stretch along the shoreline is as productive as any.

Gear: Heavy-to-medium trolling gear is preferred in the area, but it doesn't negate even the lightest of gear once the hot spots are located. There is a good race of currents just off the point of the bay and the islands to the south. Local anglers are inclined to use downriggers or heavy weights designed to take a dodger down to fair depths, using a wide variety of lures.

The hoochie or flashtail type brings good results on cohos, chinooks and pinks during July and August.

Note: The small harbour is extremely well protected, but once outside Johnstone Strait currents and winds prevail, and they can be strong. Any small car-top boat can be used with safety if normal marine precautions are adhered to in open water. Be stocked with every item you need before going into the area. Remember that heavy currents from the meeting of the Straits cause both rough and fast water.

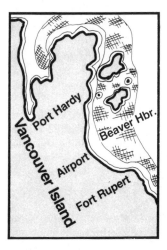

Hardy Bay
Beaver Harbour

HARDY BAY: The largest bay on the northern inside tip of Vancouver Island, it was one of the original points of human habitation on the West Coast and is the site of most early modern history and settlement. It contains the very busy and prosperous harbour of Port Hardy with a fishing fleet, fish processing plants and a good-sized town still having much of the pioneer character.

The waters of the Bay are productive and scenic right into the turbulences and weather of Queen Charlotte Sound. Clamshell middens from the native habitations line the shores and the inner bay and even extend to the uppermost point of the harbour entrances. As the Bay abuts the flow of waters from the outer and inner seas, migrations of pelagic species pass its entrance and circle into the arc between northerly Duval Island and southerly Dillon Point. Salmon are in the Bay at all seasons and excellent catches are made off the pier and float ends with casting gear. Springs are present all winter and runs of pinks and cohos move through in their more seasonal summer migratory pattern. All species of groundfish and rockfish are also there with a good clamming beach nearby.

Location: At the northernmost end of the Vancouver Island Highway, where it follows the coastline, or inside passage route, about 30 miles north of Beaver Cove. It is the more distant of excellent sports fishing areas reach-

101

Launching ramps at Telegraph Cove and Port Hardy. As the visiting
angler below has just discovered, these North Island waters
are comparatively uncrowded and productive.

able by paved highway and is rapidly becoming crowded during summer months from the influx of both B.C. and international anglers and boaters. The port has stores, accommodation, restaurants, repair shops, gas, gear and other goods. In the central harbour there is a marina and boat launching ramp. Additionally there are, alongside the main ferry landing two miles farther along the shoreline road, a pair of excellent launching ramps, side-by-side, which have car and trailer parking available.

Where to fish: About four miles long, the first section of the Bay is fairly sheltered before fanning out. Along the southerly shoreline there is a bay known as Bear Cove which is fished by local anglers for chinook salmon all year round. The centre of the Bay, on the passage outward, is also popular for chinook salmon. Much of the summertime angling is concentrated between the southerly Point Dillon and Masterman Island, where good catches of early blueback turn into fall fishing for cohos and an all-year catch for chinooks. The northerly side is somewhat less productive out to Duval Island. Most of the sports fishing begins during the nice days of March and April and extends to the middle of October, with the best catches during July and August.

Off the Gordon group of islands the southern point is a mooching hot spot, and excellent for deeply trolled lines for springs, with some coho in season. Beyond this area to Christie Pass there is good fishing, but it is not small boat water.

Gear: Local anglers tend to use the conventional medium-to-heavy trolling gear, dodger and lure. Bait can be purchased in the stores and sometimes in the fish packing plants. Strip-herring is used, but hoochie or squid-like lures are preferred. Jig-type lures are used in the central mid-Bay, also in Bear Cove. In light-gear trolling, bucktails are less common than to the south, but will produce cohos.

If you like clams, you will be in preferred territory in most of the area, and crab traps will take good-sized Dungeness specimens.

Note: Stay in the Bay to avoid rough weather. If it is rough in Hardy Bay, Beaver Harbour lies just around Dillon Point.

BEAVER HARBOUR: Not be confused with Beaver Cove, the stretch of water to the south of Hardy Bay is a large area of island-sprinkled fishing grounds which is rich in coastal beauty and variety. It was a region of early settlement, having good-sized Indian populations when the explorers started entering the top entrance to the Inland Passage. On the islands, and on the shores, can be found the remains of both former native occupations and of enterprising pioneers.

The area is an ideal coho and chinook salmon feeding ground as it is in a hook of the coastline, out of the full brunt of Queen Charlotte Strait. It is dotted with such islands as Cattle, Peel and Deer which break up the water mass to provide excellent areas for kelp. The kelp is so abundant that it once provided a local major industry. Most of the angling is done during June through September, a summer fishery more due to climatic conditions than availability of fish. It is very beautiful scenic area, with excellent possibilities of seeing seals, porpoises and other wildlife as the boat moves through the fishing grounds.

Location: Just northeast of the airport where a road leads through a modern subdivision and located in Beaver Harbour Park, there is a cement boat launching ramp. However, the whole bay is very shallow, thus the ebb tide leaves it dry for almost a quarter of a mile. Although generally hard-packed sand, it is precarious to drive on, although some do. Either a long boat carry, or a wait for high tide, is necessary to get a returning boat remounted.

The bay lies about six miles by road southeast of Hardy Bay and about the same distance around Dillon Point. All the amenities of stores, gas, lodging, meals, tackle and bait are in Port Hardy, a major commercial fishing port.

Where to fish: Moving outward from the beach launching toward Thomas Point takes the angler to a stretch below the point in the open water of Queen Charlotte Sound. Just south of Thomas Point the kelp presents visual evidence that it should be excellent for both cohos and chinooks all the way to the mouth of the Keogh River, where there was once superb Dolly Varden and some cutthroat trout angling during spring, summer and fall.

Out to Eagle Island, and on the outside, trolling is also good. At the upper channel end of Deer Island, heading toward Peel Island, a very large body of kelp becomes noticeable. Cohos can often be seen swirling along the edge of the kelp, also occasional chinooks and, in the up-cycle, some pinks. Any of this area between Deer and Peel Islands, and outwards past the rocks, or small islands, will produce salmon.

Limits of the fishin' hole may be decided by an outward circle of Peel Island, then out to the closer side of Dillon Point, then back toward Peel Island, through this passage into the bay of Beaver Harbour, always in the feeding grounds of salmon. There is productive water just inside Peel Island on the inner side of Daedalus Passage off the kelp. Perhaps defining the hole as the outskirts of the bay is the best rule to follow when seeking fish.

Gear: Any gear can be used in these waters because of the moderate depths, the proximity of fishing to kelp beds, and the lack of heavy tides in most productive fishing places. Many local anglers use trolling gear, varying from six ounces to two pounds. Bucktailing is done for cohos, but very little mooching, although it is not impossible, with fresh herring available in season at the local processing plants. Hoochie- or flashtail-type lures and spoons are excellent producers. Some strip-casting and some jig-type lure casting are done. Results are good.

Note: This area of water requires a full day to try half of the excellent places available. Any one of the points mentioned could well occupy a full afternoon or tide. Shelter is good behind the many islands and anchorage is available.

COAL HARBOUR: It is a pleasant 12-mile drive on a paved highway from Port Hardy to Coal Harbour which is one of the most northerly fishing ports of the West Coast reachable by highway. The fair-sized harbour has an historic background as a whaling and sea-plane base for the Canadian Air Force.

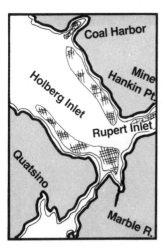

Coal Harbour

Very old, wide concrete ramps run down to the lowest tides amid the remains of old installations. There is ample parking and all free.

Location: On Holberg Inlet at the central point of three-fingered Quatsino Sound which produces excellent salmon and steelhead runs from several rivers. Major conveniences and outlets for gear and stores are at Port Hardy.

Where to fish: During winter chinook salmon can be taken right in the harbour which is moderately shallow. Off the first point, and up to Hankin Point, which is the next point southward, cohos (and pinks in their high years) can be taken. At Hankin Point, Rupert Inlet continues as a finger and has produced fish right up to its end, although less since the tailings of a mine have discolored the water.

Directly across the bay, the fast-running narrows lead to Quatsino Sound. On the southern side of the waterway the Marble River enters a long bay, and occasionally has excellent fishing at the mouth. Many craft ply these shores, reaching along Holberg Inlet which is considered by some to be the most productive side.

Faster and larger boats go out the narrows, past Drake Island and Quatsino Village to the outer section of the Sound. At this juncture the brown waters of pulp effluent from Port Alice begin to clear with flushing by the outer seas, and salmon are taken all the way out to sea. The loggers at Winter Harbour camp are very partial to fishing outward from Forward Inlet, which is nearly on the open Pacific Ocean.

Gear: The area to fish is extremely large. Trolling is the most used method, basically deep-sinking weight and lures. However, as visitors increase there is no doubt that every method from bucktailing flies to lure casting will be practiced.

Note: This is the most easily accessible of the outer West Coast distant points. There are undeveloped places for overnight camping almost anywhere. Take your own boat.

Chapter 7

WEST COAST OF VANCOUVER ISLAND
Port Alberni to Barkley Sound

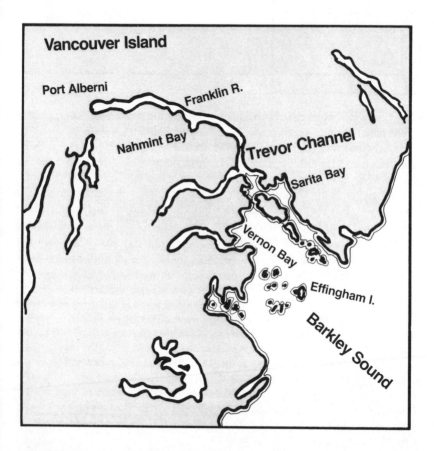

PORT ALBERNI HARBOUR: Despite the white steam and smoke hanging over Port Alberni Harbour from the pulp mill and plywood plant, and the brown liquor expelled from these installations which contributes to the cedar swamp hue of these waters, beneath them lies some of the finest large chinook salmon of the coastline. Pulp installations, well into the estuary of the Somass River system, crowded booming grounds lining the perimeter shores to the north and east, and dock fronts for deep-sea ships all provide a means of reaching the big chinooks, fishing from the booms or docks. Much of the produc-

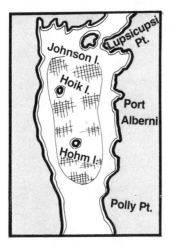

Port Alberni Harbour Boy Scout Camp

tive run is due to the early installation of upstream hatchery and fishways.

Even the extremely intensive commercial fishery which pursues the troll-caught West Coast run of immature chinooks, cohos and sockeye almost year round from the outer banks right into seining of all passages up and into Alberni Canal hasn't yet cleaned out the enhanced runs. Beginning in late July, building up through late August and on into October, the Tyee chinooks move into the Somass River and its major tributaries, the Stamp and Ash Rivers, which are fed from Sproat and Great Central Lakes. When the season of successful chinooks is on, local anglers don't mention a fish unless it breaks 25 pounds, and cohos will weigh in at 20 to 28 pounds during September.

Location: This is the deep-sea ship harbour in front of the city of Port Alberni. The crowded, small boat harbour, or yacht basin, is up the Somass River about a mile with a huge two-acre parking lot and boat launching ramp. The four-lane cement ramp goes right into the narrow river. At rush hours — dawn, dusk and after the 4:00 p.m. shift change — the ramp is busy from August to October. A smaller launching ramp in mid-Port Alberni gives more immediate access to Inner Harbour fishing.

In Port Alberni every type of service is available since it is a major center with a population of 20,000.

Where to fish: About 200 feet beyond the dredged channel of the river estuary, and out past the last marker pilings, the waters are shallow (20 to 50 feet) around both sides of the harbour, deepening to about 80 feet off Hohm Island.

Along the curve of the booms on the opposite shoreline from the city there is excellent water for trolling or using a plug which needs only two-ounces and a dodger or flasher, then around the outside of Hohm Island, over to the booms opposite the docks, then along the sheer, still-timbered coastline.

Taking the opposite tack within 50 feet in front of the docks, past the smoking plywood plant to the next marked point will be in the inward path of migrating salmon all the way. All of this water, and the entire center of

Port Alberni and its harbour. Despite log booms and pollution from the pulpmill, the harbour still yields large chinooks.

the bay between, is Tyee holding water, and can be shallow-trolled, deep-trolled or bait and lure cast with exceptional results. Believe it — to 50 pounds is possible, to 30 pounds common. Jigging the various casting lures near bottom anywhere can be productive.

Gear: Most boats troll lightly-weighted or shallow gear with dodger, herring hook-ups (Herring Magic Teaser and similar holders) round and round the harbour, but casting jig-type lures is common. There is little or no mooching or strip-casting, though strictly feasible at any time of the year.

Because of the discolored water from industrial effluents, a brighter type of attractor is practical (large dodgers, yellow herring activators, etc.) for trolling, with cut-herring preferred. Little or no bucktail-type fishing is done, either on dodger or at the surface.

Note: There is a predominant morning calm, with a local thermal draft rising before noon and often into sunset. It isn't particularly dangerous even in a 12-feet boat, but 14-feet is recommended. The chop is extremely uncomfortable.

BOY SCOUT CAMP: The beach in front of this camp is rocky and bracketed with log booms, the site of an old mine operation. Strangely enough, the waters only a few yards offshore are up to 80 feet deep. The building on the shoreline is centrally located about mid-point in the productive area of chinooks, which are traditionally sought. Here even large cohos to 20 pounds are considered to be just "another fish" by the Tyee anglers.

Location: About two miles along the southern shore of the Inlet from the inner, up-river harbour of the Alberni launching ramp and a mile from the city ramp. It is the first area past the last marker of Port Alberni Harbour, the probable closest "milling and finning" water just before the river estuary (see Port Alberni Harbour).

Where to fish: Although some anglers troll right along the inner shores of the Harbour, out past the point and down the Canal to the camp, many anglers run at speed directly to the area to begin their troll, then to Lone Tree Point and beyond. From the indentation on the Port Alberni side of the camp, out in front, then along the booms and out to 400 yards offshore, the boats circle and drop lines to over 100 feet. Springs will be shallow at dawn (30 to 50 feet), deeper at mid-day (80 to 100 feet), and up again near sundown. Cohos, in the 50-feet depths, are anywhere in the area. Salmon move in for a couple of days, and often on to the river, or they dribble past from early August to October.

Gear: This is ideal trolling-at-depth water, up to one and one-half pounds on light gear, or downriggers because the bottom is almost unobstructed by reefs, thanks to river and glacial siltation which prevents most gear from snagging.

The depths inshore where the chinooks seem to travel or form schools are perfect — 60- to 100-feet levels which allow use of casting gear, bait, or jig-type lures, and the testing of depths to find the level of the chinooks. A major terminal gear is dodger with heavy weights — drop-off type, downrigger, or slip-weights — and the larger type of planers which trip. Local anglers seldom mooch or strip-cast for chinooks but the conditions are actually ideal, with little tidal flow and sheltered in the bay. Any light casting gear will take the small tackle, heavier rods for weights, light tackle for release-type cannonball or downrigger. It isn't fly, or bucktailing water, but not impossible. It is just made difficult by the strong pollution of the inner harbour which makes the water look like swamp run-off.

Note: When the inner harbour has a strong chop, the shelter from the lee of Lone Tree Point gives some protection in the inshore waters where most chinooks are taken. It's a rough passage in a breeze.

LONE TREE POINT: The sharp pinnacle of bluffs at the Point is actually the separation boundary of the activity on either side. The waters to the down-Inlet side are exposed to the thermal updraft of the long fjord. The Port Alberni side of the point is along a rock-bound shore where booms are almost continuous, marked in numbered log compounds. It leads into a slightly-curving bay with steep sides where stiff-legs keep the booms in place, and allow the angler to fish right up to the outer logs. This is the last portion of the long Inlet on the inward salmon migration and the springs hang in close to the wall, breaking the surface on their last seaward journey before reaching the brackish waters of the Somass River estuary.

Location: The next stretch of water from the Scout Camp to the marker at Lone Tree Point. It is almost as close to China Creek as it is to Port Alberni Harbour, with the choice of launching at China Creek, Port Alberni or up the Somass River.

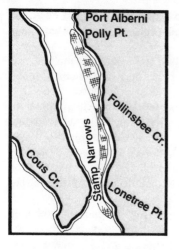

Lone Tree Point

Where to fish: The section begins with booms in which the bays are numbered, somewhere from 20 to 36, the mid-section from 30 to 34 having a slight indent into the face of the steep bluffs and timbered slopes. Possibly this is the focal point of milling salmon. Chinooks can be taken by trolling from 30- to over 100-feet depths, the more productive area at 60 to 80 feet mid-day, the lesser depths at dawn and dusk. Even when the chinooks are breaking and swirling they can be taken at 60 to 100 feet on a troll. The whole length, from the Scout Camp to the Point, and around it, is excellent trolling inshore. Boats move out to half the distance across the channel where there is shelving beach with a marker. Little effort is concentrated on the other side of the channel.

Gear: It is ideal for any type of heavy tackle, dodgers and herring activators being popular; some preference for large plugs without dodger; some planers with lures or bait. Basically, the dodger or flasher and herring in a teaser is preferable.

When the springs are there, the use of a jig-type lure is effective, being lowered progressively to bottom and moved up. Bright yellows and reds are popular, because of the darkness of the water caused by the surface pollution. Cohos are not abundant until September, and are not heavily fished for by most local anglers. Lightly-weighted tackle or bucktailing is not generally practiced. Mooching and strip-casting works, but also is seldom practiced. Tidal currents are almost unnoticeable.

Note: A good lee exists in this stretch behind the Point, but it is a rough run after the thermal draft starts up the channel.

CHINA CREEK: The waters off China Creek have long been one of the more productive salmon fishing areas of Alberni Inlet. The river, which is China Creek itself, used to have one of the finest of both summer and winter steelhead runs. Its popularity, as the first out-of-town water along the channel which was reachable by road, led to a depletion of steelhead in its clear waters. Salmon fishing, however, has remained excellent. Cohos and chinooks arrive in July-August, some chinooks earlier, and some immature springs the year round.

A new and unique sports fishery is trolling for sockeye salmon. It has become extremely productive, using flashers and pink or reddish hoochie-type gear, beginning in early July.

Location: About 10 miles south of Port Alberni on the road to Bamfield. The area of the lower stream to the foreshore is a Regional Park with a public campsite which is often crowded all summer. There are two excellent, broad ramps capable of handling even heavy traffic without a wait, with ample parking areas for cars, trucks and trailers.

Many of the anglers frequenting this area boat down the long stretch from the big ramps and facilities up the Somass River estuary. China Creek is sometimes fished as an extension of Polly Point to Lone Tree Point waters. Port Alberni has all services.

Where to fish: The bay formed to the north of the river estuary clears the estuarial sands of the river, and it drops quite quickly to 100 feet. The drop-off, along the jutting point which is the estuary itself, separates two main areas of holding water. The up-channel direction is a continuity of the Lone Tree Point fishing, with deep water.

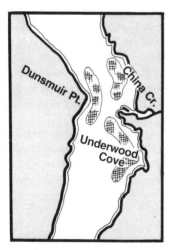

China Creek
Nahmint River

Early cohos, which are often over 15 pounds, move into the bay formed by the estuary, and can also be taken in the shallower waters. Probably the more productive water is the section down the channel into and past Underwood Cove, the next sharp hook in the land. Most of this area has excellent chinook salmon depths. It is also occasionally excellent coho waters. The land on the opposite shoreline, Dunsmuir Point, forms an eddy on either side of it for one-half mile. It can be good spring and coho fishing at times, although usually less productive than the river side.

Gear: The practice on most of the West Coast and Vancouver Island is to use heavy gear and troll. China Creek lends itself to these methods. It also shows excellent results from cast jig-type lures. Thus even the lightest rods and reels can be used, both fly- and spin-casting ones. The fact that a 20- to 50-pound spring can be taken at depth lends wisdom to the use of heavier gear. Deep planers, downriggers, fixed or drop-off one- to three-pound weights, need stiff rods and big reels, the Peetz being a favorite.

Herring slab or strip, whole or cut-plug, used in various holders such as Herring Magic and Strip Teaser, can be trolled with or without big flashers which include anything from the Abe and Al to the more modern foil-type made of plastic formed over metal. Yellow is a favored color because of the still discolored waters from the mills. Pink hootchie-type lures are best for sockeye.

Mooching and strip-casting can be effective but are not usually practiced.

Note: This water can be fished in a small boat, even a rowboat if the launching is done at China Creek. Like all of Alberni Inlet, however, it is subject to brisk winds, prevailing inward, and can become too rough to return if reached from a Somass River launching.

NAHMINT RIVER: For many years Nahmint Bay was a paradise for West Coast Tyee anglers in late summer interested primarily in catching the really big ones — 30- to 60-pounders. The river itself had one of the finest summer steelhead fisheries known anywhere. Because of its inaccessibility by road, it remained excellent until the 1960s. Latterly, with the heavy commercial seining, gill-netting and off-coast commercial fishing to which the Alberni Inlet is annually subjected, the productivity of the Nahmint River drainage has been affected. The coastline is still a virtually primitive area, with much second growth on the foreshores but with heavier, active logging now in the upper watershed. Freshetting has also greatly contributed to the depletion of the natural runs.

Location: The area was always a long run for a small boat from Port Alberni, but modern, faster motors make it a feasible one-day trip. It lies 20 miles from the Port Alberni-Somass ramp, and 10 miles from the closer China Creek launching. Rough weather in the channel can be avoided here to a greater degree than in most places, since the bay lies behind a headland which protects it from the prevailing up-channel winds.

Where to fish: In the bay itself, off the delta of Nahmint River, there is a drop-off to 100 feet, then outward to the line drawn between the points. All of this water produces chinooks and some cohos, but the major catches come in closer to the delta's drop-off.

From the inner bay out around the westerly point, all of the water is productive of larger chinooks and cohos, but the stretch for about one-third of a mile past the point, down the Inlet, seems to afford a holding area for chinooks. The height of the activity comes in mid to late August, then through September into October. The inner bay is now restricted by Federal Fisheries to all fishing after early September, usually after Labour Day. (Because fishing regulations in any region can change from season to season, always check the current *Federal Fisheries Tidal Waters Sport Fishing Guide*.)

Two popular ramps at Port Alberni
— Clutesi Haven in the community
and China Creek nine miles to the
south. During the fishing season the
ramps are busy, the reason
shown below.

Ten Mile Point, directly across the channel, has a good production record, in a semi-circle around the point. But it produces well right down to Chesnucknuw Creek and even beyond. If the weather is favorable, it is a good alternative if the Nahmint River area is slow.

Gear: Although deep-trolling is the most usual method because the big fish run predominantly in deep waters, the use of jig-type lures is also productive. Large plugs are favorite lures but slowly-trolled herring, cut or whole in holders which activate them, are equally successful in enticing the big ones. Dodgers and planers of all kinds will bring good results. Deeply-running wire lines, downriggers and drop-off weights are all also used.

Since water currents are moderate, mooching and stripping will produce results, thus lighter tackle such as mooching and spin-casting rods and reels will produce and can be used for jig-type lures. As Tyees over 30 pounds are usual, any light tackle should have lots of line capacity on the reel.

Note: While there is ample room in Nahmint Bay both for anchoring and tying up, if the weather is building for wind or fog, remember it is a long run home.

San Mateo Bay

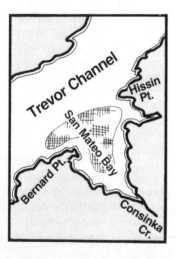

SAN MATEO BAY: This is another weekend fishing area used more by Port Alberni anglers with larger boats than by the casual small boat fisherman. It is the big bay on the south side of the Inlet's entrance, opposite Uchucklesit Inlet, in the midst of waters which have traditionally produced large commercial catches of salmon. Unfortunately, commercial fish farms for both salmon and halibut production have taken up part of the bay. Although salmon are in the Bay all year round, the area is fished more heavily in the spring to fall months. All the runs of Alberni Inlet pass it both in and out during their migrations.

Location: Some 27 miles from Port Alberni and about four miles from Poett Nook launching ramp which has wharfage, gear and a campsite. Or it is an extension of a trolling course which begins in Sarita (Numukamis) Bay, then outward around Congreve Island, Mutine and Bernard Points — the latter narrow finger being the outer seas boundary — then into a deep "V", bounded up-channel by Hissin Point. It is fished on the way to Vernon Bay or as an alternative.

Where to fish: In the inner bay, where Consinka Creek enters, depths are moderate to 120 feet with a major overall depth average of 240 feet outward from there. Any water lying inside or off Bernard and Hissin Points is both chinook salmon and coho water, with some of the biggest and brightest West Coast chinooks being taken here during all seasons. Currents are moderated, as are the winds, by surrounding land. While the run into Uchucklesit Inlet is across an area which can be choppy, once inside the Inlet the weather is less rough, with all-night anchorage available at the head.

Gear: Any gear which is normal for Sarita or Vernon Bays will take fish in San Mateo. There is some local suggestion that cast jig-type gear produces better than in the outer bays, but trolled gear, with bait or lures, is highly productive. Light gear with bait can be used, but coarse fish quickly make a meal of it.

Note: Remember, it is a four-mile run back to Poett Nook, and can be against headwinds or in fog. Otherwise, it is safe for smaller motor-equipped boats.

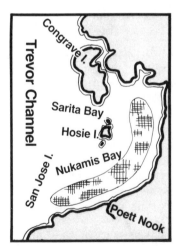

Sarita Bay

SARITA (NUMUKAMIS) BAY: Sarita Bay is one of the better known names to veteran Alberni Inlet anglers, even though on Admiralty charts it does not exist. The real name of the waters encompassed by Congreve Island in the inland direction of Trevor Channel and to Nanat Island on the ocean side is Numukamis Bay. The Sarita River, once an excellent salmon and steelhead stream, pushes its delta centrally into the bend, and is responsible for some of the excellent year-round salmon fishing.

Poett Nook, with its modern campsite, wharfage and launching ramp, is the logical small boat entrance to the large area of fishing, and is an integral part of the large bay. Many Port Alberni sport fishermen run down by boat and use Sarita as a weekend trip focal point, about a 30-mile run.

Location: From the inner harbour of Poett Nook — one of the many almost totally land-locked harbours of the greatly fragmented West Coast — the outer waters are only about 200 yards. Fishing can begin even in the small harbour.

Bamfield lies five miles farther down the channel toward the Pacific Ocean, and it is a major fishing port. As such, it has some accommodation, boat rental, stores, gear, and other services. Small boat cartoppers can find accesses along the shoreline by way of logging roads, and by carrying their outfit to the tideline.

Where to fish: The bay is nearly three miles long on the shoreline. Inner Poett Nook has chinooks during midwinter and herring which can at times be jigged. Once out of its confines, however, a line can go down from 60 to 240 feet while still quite close to shore, and also be into a chinook, coho or sockeye, as well as an exceptional number of rockfish, sea bass, lings and red snappers.

Chinook can be taken at any time of the year from the more seaward point of Nanat Island to the outward curvature of Congreve Island where Trevor Channel bends toward Port Alberni. Off centrally-located Santa Maria Island the waters tend to shallow, then blend with the delta of Sarita River which has a quick drop-off. From here, along to the outer shores of Congreve Island, coho fishing is best in the summer and early fall months.

Gear: Much of the salmon fishing is done with deep troll methods ranging from large planers and heavy drop-, or lift-off weights, to downriggers. Terminal tackle is dodger and lures, or cut bait with the Herring Magic type of strip, or whole herring activator. Jig-type lure casting is a recognized method and is being more persistently used. Mooching and strip-casting with fresh bait (herring or anchovies can be jigged or raked at times) is almost instantly interfered with by the abundance of coarse fish (rockfish, lingcod, sea bass, red snapper, etc.) before the line can get to a required depth.

Light-weight tackle, such as mooching, strip-casting, threadline and fly gear will work, and will take fish, the more energetic West Coast salmon testing it to the limit. If fillets from sea bass, snapper and rockfish are desirable, a meal can be caught in no time.

Note: This area is generally shielded by the bulk of Tzartus and Fleming Islands and by the circumference of the bay from outer seas weather, but it can get rough and fog will roll in quite suddenly. It is, however, one of the safer small boat waters on this rugged Outer Coast.

SATELLITE PASSAGE: When a craft leaves Bamfield Inlet outward bound in a westerly direction, the land of the Deer Island group seems to form a solid boundary, with Satellite Passage as the only possible break. The Pass lies between two major points, Helby and Sandford Islands, with the fairly

Satellite Passage

Imperial Eagle Ch
Fleming I.
Sandford I.
Satellite Passage
Helby I.
Diana I.

small Wizard Islets more or less centered in the entrance to the Passage.

Since the undersea ridge is continuous, Satellite Passage is a mass of underwater pockets and reefs. Such conditions create a good flow of tidal currents and form an ideal habitat for small fish, bait and ground fish, also an entrance for migrating fish from one sound or inlet to the next. There are always salmon in the area — anything from cohos and chinook grilse to maturing fish, with an excellent sports fishery for sockeye, using a pink hootchie behind a dodger or flasher. The sockeye fishing begins in mid to late June.

Since Satellite is a passage to the outer seas via the broad open waters of Imperial Eagle Channel, anglers should remember that once on the outside to the west, the next stop is the Orient!

Location: From Poett Nook launching and campsite, the trip is about five miles; from the inner harbour ramps of Bamfield, it is under two miles. Bamfield has almost any service an angler may require.

Where to fish: After crossing Trevor Channel from the southerly Vancouver Island mainland, the first small islands, Wizard Islets, are quite apparent in the channel. Just northwest of them, the main channel shows distinct tidal currents, while depths diminish to as little as 50 feet.

If a boat is allowed to drift or travel at low speed, signs of feed are evident when the waters are calm. A glance over the side often reveals anchovies swimming in fairly large schools. If the water is choppy, the number of murres, murrelets, shags, or cormorants, and wheeling and diving gulls, will indicate such feed. A jig-line cast over, or into, will produce fresh bait in fair quantities. This is one West Coast area where mooching, strip-casting and drift-mooching will bring excellent results.

The Trevor Channel approach to the waters of Satellite Passage seems to be more consistently holding water for bait and salmon than those of outer Imperial Eagle Channel, but the flow of the tide can alter this condition. A circular course in and around Wizard Islets, through the passage and out, with

Launching at Grice Bay, a protected waterway near the north
end of Pacific Rim National Park.
The Broken Group of islands at the entrance to Barkley Sound. This
region, exposed to the full force of the Pacific Ocean with
Japan the nearest land, is not water for car-top boats.

a similar pattern made on the outside in Imperial Eagle Channel, will keep lines in the more productive waters.

Gear: This area is one of the best for light tackle on the coast, mooching, strip-casting and jig-lure casting producing good results. However, it is a tackle-grabber for anything which hits bottom. Knowledge of the passage will allow any type of deep troll, but the varying depths have to be considered at all times. It isn't an ideal downrigger, or heavily-weighted lure area, because of the changeable depths. Dodgers with lures or bait of any kind will work successfully if used carefully and with reference to the depth-sounder or charts.

Note: As is the case with all the outer West Coast, unless equipped with dual power and marine radio, it is dangerous water for the newcomer. Go equipped — or don't go!

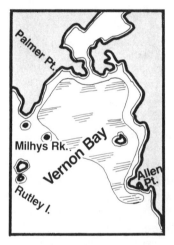

Vernon Bay

VERNON BAY: The big bay lies on the northwest tip of Barclay Sound. It isn't the farthest west fishin' hole to which the sports angler goes, but if you go farther and your boat stalls, the next stop is Asia. It is a large bay with enough holes to handle many boats without crossing lines. It has a year-round fishing potential — early bluebacks and chinook salmon to late fall mature fish, and anchovies in enough abundance to jig most days.

Location: It is about 42 miles from the Somass River Marina at Alberni, with the closest launching ramp at Poett Nook. Then it is six miles by fairly open water to Vernon Bay. The closest services are at Poett Nook, with Bamfield and Alberni next. Recent improvements and changes in Bamfield have added several fish guiding outfits and two launching ramps, adequate for trailered boats, one centrally in Bamfield and another nearby at Seabeam Marina.

Where to fish: Any part of the circumference between Allen and Palmer Points will produce chinooks and cohos, and the largest variety of rockfish, lingcod, sole and flounder any angler could wish for. Mid-bay produces bluebacks or cohos most of the year, the bulk of the chinooks coming from the inshore areas. Feed is visible at almost any time of the tide or day, almost always registering on the depth-finder. The ever-present diving birds — murres, murrelets and cormorants — indicate the hidden bait-fish, with diving gulls a sure sign. Salmon are often beneath the feed, 30 to 50 feet for cohos, 80 to 150 for chinooks. The centre section of the bay and outward several hundred yards from shore is a common trolling pattern. The close-in rock coastline produces chinooks.

Gear: Most Vernon Bay anglers troll, the average weight being one pound or better, using a dodger with a herring activator, or planers of the larger size with bait or lure. Bucktails, hoochies and similar lures will work well, as do plugs and spoons.

Downriggers, or line with weight-releases, work very effectively, as do the infrequently used lift-off drop-weights. The tides are not too strong, but the fish apparently live deeper than on the inside passage. It is seldom done, but live bait can be had by jigging the abundant anchovies, then mooching with 2- to 10-ounce swivel weights. While strip-casting isn't common, jig-type lure casting is and yields well on chinooks in the 20- to 30-pound class, as well as immature ones. Cohos respond to these methods as well.

Note: If a black line shows on any horizon, it is a good time to get out. Don't go there without a secondary motor, and/or at least a good CB radio.

EFFINGHAM ISLAND: For the adventurous or well-qualified skipper, the run out to Effingham Island is an extension of borders from Vernon Bay or Satellite Passage fishing. It is a long way out, at the border of the wide open Pacific Ocean, and is as wonderfully scenic as this island-fragmented coastline can be. It is also treacherous, part of a region known as the "Graveyard of the Pacific." Among scores of vessels wrecked was the *Vanlene*. She was a large, modern transport ship which hit the rocks, her cargo hundreds of cars. The wreck for many years was a landmark but has now disappeared. Beyond her burial place there is a spattering of small islands, then wide open sea.

Location: Roughly 13 miles from Vernon Bay, Bamfield and Poett Nook, at the edge of the Pacific Ocean, Effingham Island is twice as large as a dozen surrounding smaller islands and a host of reefhead islets. There is a

Anglers should treat Barkley Sound with great respect. The *Vanlene* was one of scores of vessels which have been wrecked on the Sound's reefs and rocks.

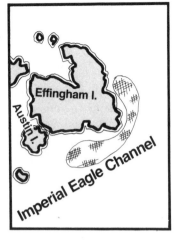

Effingham Island

sheltering harbour on the inner side of Effingham facing into Coaster Channel. A craft going out to this point should have either dual motors or reliable radio and a knowledgeable seaman aboard. Not only are the reefs numerous around it, but the fogs are impenetrable and the seas not too predictable. There are no nearby stores, fueling depots, or public services.

Where to fish: The focal point for most sports craft to begin fishing is Meares Bluff which is the inner corner on Imperial Eagle Channel. If the weather is unsettled, try the inside face leading into Coaster Channel, and when the weather is calm the outer face which leads to the open Pacific and out to Cree Island. Along the inner face the waters have a shelf which runs from 50 to 120 feet and has a tendency to hold both bait-fish and cohos. The outer face and out to Cree is deeper water, but is also excellent coho territory. These are some of the most active salmon to be caught anywhere, usually upward of 10 pounds during the summer. Perhaps the vicinity of the point of Meares Bluff is the best all-round fishing water.

Gear: West Coast tackle is generally heavy trolling or deep-running gear, dodgers or flashers with hoochie or squid-type lures. Few anglers bother to jig, net or even bring fresh bait, but anchovies can be seen near the surface in most of these waters and are prime bait. Thus, a light-hued fly, grey and white, is quite effective when trolled either with dodger or up to four ounces of weight.

The seas are open, rolling as a rule, and tend to give good action to any lure. Casting lures produce fair results, better if the angler knows his areas of fish concentration or passage. As the salmon are usually larger than in inner waters, more line on the reel is logical, as is higher test leader.

Note: Effingham Island is a last stop on the way to the Orient, and borders the open Pacific Ocean. As already noted, it is subject to wind and fog, and strong tidal currents. Radio communication, and dual motor power, as well as knowledge of the sea, should be necessities — or don't go out there! Even better, run with a partner craft.

Chapter 8

WEST COAST OF VANCOUVER ISLAND
Ucluelet to Fair Harbour

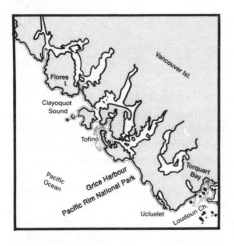

**Tofino
Ucluelet
Grice Harbour
Pacific Rim Park**

VANCOUVER ISLAND WEST COAST — GENERAL: I have fished much of the West Coast in a small boat, and some of it in larger craft, too. However, in this book I have limited description to the particular areas which are described as fishin' holes, of which I have enough personal experience to give detailed and useful knowledge. It is easy to generalize and be correct on a percentage basis, but knowing a more exact position at which to begin actual fishing, derived from personal catch records, gives the incoming angler more probability of catching fish, and more confidence about going.

Otherwise, one could point offshore anywhere in British Columbia and say: "Go out there in June, October, January or March, put your line in the water with something on it that glitters or darts, and you will catch fish." And, on a percentage basis, this statement is the truth.

Thus, although having both fished and caught salmon and coarse fish at the following areas, I have judged it better to treat them from the standpoint of personal knowledge alone.

TOFINO: The community of Tofino is worth the drive just for a visit. It is a major fishing port of Vancouver Island with a picturesque, rugged, rock-faced inner harbour on Browning Passage at the entrance to Tofino Inlet. The outer side of Tofino village is the open Pacific Ocean. The harbour is filled with deep-sea fishing craft and has canneries and fish packing, sorting and freezing facilities.

Because of the excellent, if winding, highway, a large increase in tourism, mainly spring, summer and early fall months, has resulted in excellent fishing charter and marina type services, first class accommodation, and sightseeing trips for whale-watching, etc. There is a commercial sector strongly catering to visiting anglers.

Location: Follow Highway 4 west from Port Alberni approximately 60 miles to a major junction. To the right 20 miles is Tofino; to the left 5 miles is Ucluelet. Tofino has every convenience one could expect of an outpost fishing port, as well as a fair public launching ramp but with very little close-by parking.

Where to fish: Rounding the point outward-bound is the open sea with a sprinkle of small islands offshore. Inshore fishing is excellent for cohos and coarse fish, from Vargas Island southeast to Cox Point. It isn't protected, except for the lee of a couple of islands, and is not the place for a novice to venture alone. Local anglers fish this stretch, as well as Tofino Inlet.

Gear: The areas are miles long, the gear subject to knowledge of the reef-and-island dotted waters, but any trolling gear will take fish. Light tackle isn't generally used, but will produce just as it will anywhere on the coast.

Note: You would be advised to have a local angler with you if you venture outside Tofino Inlet. Also fishing will be even better on the inner waters with some local assistance.

GRICE HARBOUR: On the highway to Tofino, about midway (10 miles) in either direction from the Port Alberni Highway junction there is a rather incongruous road sign which announces a golf course, and a branch road leading approximately northeast. After passing the golf course, there is a nearly three-mile-long paved road leading to a dead end which is known as Grice Harbour about midway in Grice Bay. There is a boat ramp of good quality with ample parking but no services.

Location: As designated in the preceding paragraph.

Where to fish: This is a large, inland bay well protected from the extremities of the outer ocean. It is, nevertheless, subject to winds off the Pacific Ocean, but has many bays with shelter. There are noticeable large tidal flats and several river entries. The salmon fishing is mainly later than the outer oceanic fishing but reported to be seasonally good at or near river mouths.

Gear: Traditional trolling, casting gear with less of the deep-water type.

Note: This area is much more sheltered than the open seas. At the boat launching ramp there is no camping permitted (the sign says), but about 20 good bays exist for cars, trucks with trailers, and one toilet. A sign at the launching ramp warns against eating shellfish from the inlet since the area is reported to be subject to "red tide" of the West Coast.

PACIFIC RIM PARK (Long Beach Unit): Major development has occurred on the Pacific coastline for about 25 miles, beach parking crowded at

The West Coast fishing and logging community of Tofino. It and neighboring Ucluelet are becoming increasingly popular with sports fishermen.

most entry points, and many tourist facilities booked ahead during summer months. Occasional beach casting is done along the whole sea coast, mainly for coarse fish, but heavy swells make surf boarding more practicable, and it is the more common recreation.

UCLUELET: Almost a twin fishing port with Tofino, Ucluelet is a long-established village with a good harbour. There is a concrete ramp, all services, stores and conveniences. Paved access to this Pacific Coast has brought extreme improvement in tourist facilities, which include several top-rated (some top-priced) charter and guiding services. In mid-town there is a public launching ramp, but it is a bit narrow with little nearby parking for trailers and cars. While local marina space is crowded, newer facilities are under consideration.

Location: On Ucluelet Inlet, via Loudoun Channel. When good weather is expected, larger craft reach the Channel by crossing Imperial Eagle Channel via Sechart Channel. By vehicle it is five scenic miles to Ucluelet from the main junction of Highway 4 from Port Alberni.

Where to fish: Although deep-sea salmon fleets operate out in the ocean from Ucluelet, Toquart Bay, at the head of Loudoun Channel, has long been known as the sport fishing spot. The run used to be made by small craft from Ucluelet, but logging road access is now available from the Highway 4 near Kennedy Lake. The Bay is relatively shallow, 50 to 120 feet, with the shoreline lying between Snowden Island and the mainland being the favorite spot. Toquart River produces good salmon and steelhead runs and the mouth of the river provides excellent coho fishing from as early as June.

Gear: While depths are not extreme in most of the bay, deep troll patterns of fishing are favored. Any of the lures applicable to Alberni Inlet are productive in Toquart Bay. Light tackle is not usually the method used, but it will take salmon well in the inner areas.

Note: It is remote, but fairly sheltered by both the Broken Islands Group out to sea and Vancouver Island mainland. It is not an area to be approached by sea in small boats.

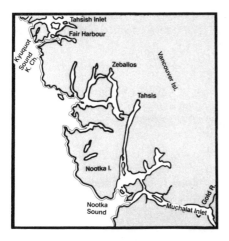

Gold River
Zeballos
Tahsis
Fair Harbour

GOLD RIVER: Before the installation of the big Gold River pulp mill, the waters off the mouth of the river were one of the best salmon grounds in the world. Subsequent devastating logging methods denuded the watersheds of Gold River and dredged out the gravels of the Heber, Muchalat and Gold Rivers, leaving canyons of boulders where pools used to brim with salmon, thus practically destroying the fish runs.

It was a common daily pastime, when an angler launched from the Gold River beach on the local waterfront Indian Reserve, to troll in front of the deltas and boat several 25- to 70-pound chinooks in a day. Much of this formerly excellent stretch of water is now fronted by the millsite and covered by booms. The Federal Fisheries Department took its usual tardy steps and incorporated restrictions against sports fishing which cut off the bulk of that productive fishing time near the river mouth. It is right that such restrictions make an attempt to prevent the total loss of the salmon, but it would be more sensible if commercial fishing was more restricted to seaward.

The days of the enormously large spring salmon, the common 50 to 60 pounders coming into small boats almost every time out in July and August are gone.

There is fishing in the inlet, but it has a restricted entrance to it along a narrow road which has a fair ramp beside it. However, the road is always completely occupied by cars and trucks. It isn't easy to park a trailer anywhere nearby. There is a public campsite, and a private one, in the vicinity of the town of Gold River, eight miles back up the highway, where there is a tackle store as well as other provisions.

Where to fish: The waters facing along the river estuary still produce salmon when they are not subject to closure. Local anglers run out to Victor Island, a good evening run, or down to Gore Island waters about 16 miles away. They consider it the best fishing area.

Gear: Anything which takes salmon in Alberni Inlet will also take them in Muchalat Inlet.

Note: Thermal drafts cause an almost daily rough-water condition beginning right in front of the river estuary. It isn't really a small boat area, 14 feet being minimum.

ZEBALLOS — TAHSIS — FAIR HARBOUR: These three areas are accessible by logging roads, either by way of Gold River, Nimpkish or Woss Camp, and are worth the effort to get there. Another approach is from Campbell River north to Sayward then to Woss Camp and on.

TAHSIS: It is at the head of Tahsis Inlet, which is a long narrow fjord reaching from Nootka Sound, (which in turn abuts Muchalat Inlet) and is a town with logging as the main interest. It is not a fishing center but is about the same distance as Zeballos from the entrance to Esperanza Inlet.

ZEBALLOS: It is also a logging town and port, but was the site of a once well-known gold mine, and is situated near an excellent steelhead river, which contributes to the local salmon populations. The multi-fractured coastline leads out to salmon fishing, where local anglers make good use of the outer reaches of the inlets.

FAIR HARBOUR: Along a gravel logging road 15 miles west of Zeballos, this historic townsite has a dirt and gravel launching site, not a ramp. It is best to bring everything needed for at least a three-day trip, which will be just about enough time to get you interested in one of the more remote fishing spots of the coastline. Because Kyuquot Sound, where the site is located, is a corral-like enclosure, blocked off from the main surge of the outer seas by Union Island, waters are moderately calm.

Where to fish: Much of the sports catch comes from the waters between Vancouver Island and the stretch around Moketas and Hohoae Islands, but the entrances on either side of Union Island which lead to the open seas are productive of commercial catches.

Gear: (See ALBERNI and GOLD RIVER sections).

Note: As approach is on logging roads, the companies which control the access should be contacted before entering. Stay within their rules and stay out of trouble.

A selection of other HERITAGE HOUSE titles:

Heritage House books are sold throughout Western Canada. If not available — or for a free 16-page catalogue listing 150 titles — write: Heritage House, Box 1228, Station A, Surrey, B.C. V3S 2B3. Shipped postpaid in Canada. Payment can be by cheque or money order.

The PIONEER DAYS IN BRITISH COLUMBIA Series

Every article is true, many written or narrated by those who, 100 or more years ago, lived the experiences they relate. Each volume contains 160 pages in large format magazine size (8½ x 11″), four-color covers, some 60,000 words of text and over 200 historical photos, many published for the first time.

A continuing Canadian best seller in four volumes which have sold over 75,000 copies. Each volume, $8.95

WHITE SLAVES OF THE NOOTKA

On March 22, 1803, while anchored in Nootka Sound on the West Coast of Vancouver Island, the *Boston* was attacked by "friendly" Nootka Indians. Twenty-five of her 27 crew were massacred, their heads "arranged in a line" for survivor John Jewitt to identify. Jewitt and another survivor became 2 of 50 slaves owned by Chief Maquina, never knowing what would come first — rescue or death.

The account of their ordeal, published in 1815, remains remarkably popular. New Western Canadian edition, well illustrated. 128 pages. $8.95

LOWER MAINLAND BACKROADS:

This best selling series contains complete information from Vancouver to the southern Cariboo. Each volume contains mile-by-mile route mileage, history, fishing holes, wildlife, maps, photos and much other information.

Volume One — Garibaldi to Lillooet, Bridge River Country. $9.95
Volume Two — The Fraser Valley. $2.95
Volume Three — Junction Country: Boston Bar to Clinton. $9.95

OUTLAWS AND LAWMEN OF WESTERN CANADA

These true police cases prove that our history was anything but dull. Chapters in 160-page Volume Three, for instance, include Saskatchewan's Midnight Massacre, The Yukon's Christmas Day Assassins, When Guns Blazed at Banff, and Boone Helm — The Murdering Cannibal.

Each of the three volumes in this Canadian best seller series is well illustrated with maps and photos and four-color photos on the covers. Volume One, $7.95; Volume Two, $7.95; Volume Three, $9.95

B.C. PROVINCIAL POLICE STORIES: Mystery and Murder from the Files of Western Canada's First Lawmen

The B.C. Police, born in 1858, were the first lawmen in Western Canada. During their 90 years of service they established a reputation as one of the most progressive police forces in North America. All cases in this best selling title are reconstructed from archives and police files by ex-Deputy Commissioner Cecil Clark who served on the force for 35 years.

Sixteen chapters, many photos. 128 pages. $7.95

THE DEATH OF ALBERT JOHNSON: Mad Trapper of Rat River

Albert Johnson in 1932 triggered the greatest manhunt in Canada's Arctic history. In blizzards and numbing cold he was involved in four shoot-outs, killing one policeman and gravely wounding two other men before being shot to death.

This revised, enlarged edition includes photos taken by "Wop" May, the legendary bush pilot whose flying skill saved two lives during the manhunt. Another Canadian best seller. $7.95

FORT STEELE: Here History Lives

From a thriving 1890s community that called itself "The Capital of the Kootenays," Fort Steele declined to a ghost town. But it was reprieved when the B.C. Government began a restoration program which now attracts some 300,000 visitors a year.

Here in 50,000 words with over 100 photos and four-color covers, Fort Steele lives again. 160 pages. $9.95

TRAGEDIES OF THE CROWSNEST PASS

In Canada no place equals the tragedies which have buffeted the Crowsnest Pass on the B.C.-Alberta border. At Frank a mountain collapsed, killing nearly 100 people; at nearby Hillcrest 189 miners died in a mine disaster; at Fernie another explosion killed 128 miners and a massive fire left virtually every resident homeless.

Revised edition of a Canadian best seller. 96 pages. $6.95

THE BEST OF B.C.'s HIKING TRAILS

Here are 20 great hikes from all around B.C. to suit hikers of all levels of ability. Each hike is accurately described and mapped and you'll find complete details of how to get there and what you can expect to find.

Illustrated throughout with photographs, this is essential reading for all hiking enthusiasts. 174 pages. $9.95

An Explorer's Guide: MARINE PARKS OF B.C.

To tens of thousands of boaters, B.C.'s Marine Parks are as welcome and convenient as their popular highway equivalents. This guide includes anchorages and onshore facilities, trails, picnic areas, campsites, history and other information. In addition, it is profusely illustrated with color and black and white photos, maps and charts.

Informative reading for boat owners from runabouts to cabin cruisers. 200 pages. $12.95

GO FISHING WITH THESE BEST SELLING TITLES

HOW TO CATCH SALMON — BASIC FUNDAMENTALS

The most popular salmon book ever written. Information on trolling, rigging tackle, most productive lures, proper depths, salmon habits, how to play and net your fish, downriggers, where to find fish.

Sales over 120,000. 176 pages. $4.95

HOW TO CATCH SALMON — ADVANCED TECHNIQUES

The most comprehensive advanced salmon fishing book available. Over 200 pages crammed full of how-to tips and easy-to-follow diagrams. Covers all popular salmon fishing methods: mooching, trolling with bait, spoons and plugs, catching giant chinook, and much more.

A continuing best seller. 256 pages. $8.95

HOW TO CATCH CRABS: How popular is this book? This is the 10th printing. 114 pages. $3.50

HOW TO CATCH BOTTOMFISH: Revised and expanded. $4.95

HOW TO CATCH SHELLFISH: Updated 4th printing. 144 pages. $3.95

HOW TO CATCH TROUT by Lee Straight, one of Canada's top outdoorsmen. 144 pages. $4.95

HOW TO COOK YOUR CATCH: Cooking seafood on the boat, in a camper or at the cabin. 7th printing. 192 pages. $3.95

FLY FISH THE TROUT LAKES: Everything you need to know about fly fishing B.C.'s lakes by Jack Shaw, a master angler who lives at Kamloops in B.C.'s famous trout country. Well illustrated. $7.95